MW01254025

John Maynard Keynes and the Economy of Trust

DOI: 10.1057/9781137467232.0001

Also by Donatella Padua

TRUST, SOCIAL RELATIONS AND ENGAGEMENT: **Understanding Customer Behaviour on the Web**

DOI: 10.1057/9781137467232.0001

palgrave▸pivot

John Maynard Keynes and the Economy of Trust: The Relevance of the Keynesian Social Thought in a Global Society

Donatella Padua

PhD in the Science of Education, Senior Researcher in Sociology and Adjunct Professor of Methods of Analysis of the Complex Society, Università per Stranieri di Perugia, Italy

palgrave
macmillan

DOI: 10.1057/9781137467232.0001

First published 2014 by
PALGRAVE MACMILLAN

Palgrave Macmillan in the UK is an imprint of Macmillan Publishers Limited, registered in England, company number 785998, of Houndmills, Basingstoke, Hampshire RG21 6XS.

Palgrave Macmillan in the US is a division of St Martin's Press LLC, 175 Fifth Avenue, New York, NY 10010.

Palgrave Macmillan is the global academic imprint of the above companies and has companies and representatives throughout the world.

Palgrave® and Macmillan® are registered trademarks in the United States, the United Kingdom, Europe and other countries.

ISBN: 978-1-137-46724-9   EPUB
ISBN: 978-1-137-46723-2   PDF
ISBN: 978-1-137-46722-5   Hardback

A catalogue record for this book is available from the British Library.

Library of Congress Cataloging-in-Publication Data

Padua, Donatella.
    John Maynard Keynes and the economy of trust : the relevance of the Keynesian social thought in a global society / Donatella Padua.
        pages cm
    ISBN 978-1-137-46722-5 (hardback)
        1. Trust – Economic aspects. 2. Consumer behavior – Psychological aspects. 3. Keynesian economics. 4. Keynes, John Maynard, 1883–1946. I. Title.

BJ1500.T78P33 2014
330.15'6—dc23   2014034467

www.palgrave.com/pivot

DOI: 10.1057/9781137467232

to Giorgio

DOI: 10.1057/9781137467232.0001

Contents

DOI: 10.1057/9781137467232.0001

DOI: 10.1057/9781137467232.0001

Foreword

Confidence passes through the rediscovery of Keynes

The strength and courage of Donatella Padua's book resides in its facing an extremely delicate issue in the midst of a deep crisis of both our economy and system. To talk about confidence within a *capitalist economy* requires an attentive consideration of its meanings and of the relationships it encourages, measuring from time to time the fear of making steps back as well as the certainty of succeeding.

▶

In political economy university courses, students are explained that confidence is one of the fundamental variables to keep the system together and to favour its growth. Confidence can be considered a melting pot of immaterial elements which influence our consumption, saving and investment decisions. This confidence, in Italy, is currently at its lowest point. It is since August 2011 that the Istat indicator on the confidence of Italian families has been decreasing inexorably and it has reached its lowest level since the year it was calculated for the first time, that is, since 1996. In this context it is not the case to talk about lack of confidence because this concept has in itself 'an intrinsic economic value' capable of damaging further consumption and the investments that would be technically sustainable. Common people think that in certain circumstances it is preferable to save rather than to spend because worse times could come, and they become therefore extremely cautious. Confidence encourages us to spend, while fear drives us to save. Perhaps this is not

DOI: 10.1057/9781137467232.0002

a 'pondered' attitude, for it is rather an irrational reaction to the crisis in the attempt of sheltering ourselves from an event that touches us as individuals, families and enterprises.

To fully understand the meaning of confidence, we need to have an indestructible certainty of what is our future. The most beautiful and significant example I know of is the story of Florentino Ariza in Gabriel Garcia Marquez's masterpiece 'Love in the Time of Cholera'. It is a story which lasts 53 years, 7 months and 11 days (nights included) and in this long period the main character never stops believing that sooner or later he will achieve his objective. It is a sociological work capable of explaining better than anything else what is the confidence in life of a common person.

Coming back to the topic of this Preface, to rediscover Lord John Maynard Keynes is an act of courage, as is also the comeback of Keynesian policies. Let me try and explain.

Keynes hated revolutionaries and he did not love reactionaries. He was far from thinking that the optimism of the former, who believed in a radical turning upside down of the system, would have prevailed; but he equally refused the pessimism of the latter, for they wanted to keep the status quo, in their opinion too dangerous to change or simply affect in any way.

In our times much caution is required to place oneself in the middle. In times in which the *adoration* for GDP and development models based on the wildest neoliberal policies prevail, to attempt the introduction of restrictions is an operation of great economic, political and cultural relevance. In the fight between State and market, the market has won by far to the detriment of any State intervention with the aim of reducing social differences.

Today Keynes is out of standard. In other words, he is out of fashion. I imagine that a man like him would be very disappointed to discover that his teachings have been so short-lived. From this point of view, the battle over the resistance of the various development models has been won by Adam Smith. Development at all cost is based on the policies encouraged by the so-called 'animal spirits' instead of on the introduction of precise rules to regulate offer and demand. The idea of freedom has widely trespassed that of responsibility, now little considered and respected. 'Yet, freedom – writes Padua [see Concluding Remarks] – lives, thanks to its opposition to the concept of constraint and restriction.' The Rhenish model of capitalism, attentive to the distribution of wealth, has given way to the far more aggressive Anglo-Saxon model, based instead on the accumulation of wealth. This is what has been happening for the last three decades or even more. This is the reason we have entered an epochal crisis. This – I suppose – is the reason which will bring *capitalism to have a limited duration* (G. Ruffolo, *Il capitalismo ha i secoli contati*, Einaudi, Torino, 2009).

Of the three social paradigms concerning the concept of confidence in economy summarized by Padua, the first one has taken root considerably and it is the *deregulated model*. This leaves plenty of room for the intervention of investment banks and rating agencies. The second one is instead the *centralized model*, where confidence is canalized towards only one central organization, though always within the dynamics of a free market. Finally, the third model resembles the second one with the variation that confidence is regulated by an ample *parterre* of institutional bodies.

Ideas to change direction exist, but nobody embraces them. Yet the incentives provided by modern research – even though the sources are really disparate – allow us to rethink the sense and the direction of their development. Let us consider some of them in scattered order.

The social doctrine of the Catholic Church offers important occasions to rediscover the importance of the individual in contrast with the importance of finance. Starting from the *Rerum Novarum* (1891) up to the *Caritas in Veritate* (2009) there have been explicit condemnations. The second encyclical letter states that a mercantile logic cannot be extended to solve social problems. It then highlights how in the relationship between enterprise and ethics there is no possibility to address efficaciously the future of mankind. It also stresses the need to manage profit so that it can favour the 'humanization of the market' and of our society. From the point of view we are interested in here, the official document of the Church observes: 'Without internal forms of solidarity and mutual trust, the market cannot completely fulfil its economic function. And today it is this trust which has ceased to exist, and the loss of trust is a grave loss' (Pope Benedict XVI, 2009, p. 55).

The fact is that a market economy genetically needs a certain amount of underdevelopment and poverty to be able to work well. It expresses itself through the incredible and self-evident truth that the system does not allow everybody to find employment; as a consequence, a percentage of the workforce is redundant, or as we say today, in excess. For those in this condition there is no collective recognition. They are just

DOI: 10.1057/9781137467232.0002

unemployed. They have an identity based on diversity, that you can see against the light.

In this case, the capitalist system has fed itself with fear rather than with confidence: The fear to see ourselves associated with the socially excluded pushes us to surround ourselves with status symbols which are often well beyond our means. We do this to belong to a winning social identity.

A wide range of famous scholars, among whom Hannah Arendt, Amartya Sen, Edgar Morin, Martha C. Nussbaum and Serge Latouche, have declared to be against Gross Domestic Product (GDP) and the inevitability of the fact that some people are happier than others. To the same category belong also Zymunt Bauman and the young and easy David Graeber, one of the leaders of the movement 'Occupy Wall Street'.

Even though there are great differences between them, their contributions share the desire to place human beings at the centre of the system; to introduce correctives to an economic situation which favours a small minority to the detriment of the rest of the population (that is the majority); to reconsider from its foundations the domination of GDP and to look for other parameters of evaluation to measure people's wealth with their stories and expectations. In brief, with all necessary caution, we can say that these scholars are the offspring of Keynesianism – a Keynesianism to be interpreted as a cultural *milieu* which is trying to limit the damage caused by a model based on the division of wealth, power and knowledge.

It is also what Nussbaum means when he writes that 'the real purpose of development is human development'. It seems obvious, but it is not really so. The elementary logic of simple and accessible reasoning does not always coincide with econometric models and with the need of enterprises to accelerate competitiveness and productivity. The priority is to produce as many goods as possible in the littlest amount of time. This has three consequences: (a) that we do not know what to do with all these products; (b) employment goes down vertically because competitiveness reduces the cost of the labour factor; (c) the wealth of an individual is now measured, for example, on the number of shoes or shirts he/she has in his/her wardrobe.

In her books Nussbaum indicates a series of pre-conditions thanks to which a person can go back to being the purpose and not the means by which half of mankind is flooded with products. The main meaning of these pre-conditions is to give sense to the indicators which measure

DOI: 10.1057/9781137467232.0002

the individual quality of life. Central must be the human ability and possibility to interact with others. The case of China is enlightening. In this country GDP is rising at breakneck speed, but we cannot say the same thing for its single citizens, if we think about their political rights in terms of freedom of thought and speech. The Chinese will never have 'the freedom to do something' until they will not have the time to plan it out.

The excessive power of ambitious financial experts and their self-confident forays must not make us underestimate the social and cultural relevance of human relationships, which are the main way to bring to the foreground the individual and his/her needs. Confused, as we are, by the principle of economic growth at all cost and by 'just in time' accounting logics, I like the idea of recalling an alternative way to interpret the world, the way expressed by John Donne, who already at the beginning of the seventeenth century put down these words: 'No man is an island entire of itself, everybody is a piece of the continent, a part of the main.'

Sen, a clever scholar of social and economic issues, follows the same semantic path and suggests to render the human factor central in the relationship with social phenomena. He does not hesitate to criticize the capitalist economic system on the negative forms of freedom, that is the 'freedom from' (for instance, from exploitation) to then affirm the fundamental right to be 'free to' (for example, to choose). Among other things, he stresses how the convulsive rhythm of modern society represents the new normality and how this prevents us from dedicating time to wellness as time addressed to the capability of being and doing. In other words, it does not allow us to see a perspective that goes beyond the attention given to income or to competitive growth at all cost. The neo-liberalistic system continues to make us think that happiness is measured on the basis of personal income (or on the fact that one's SUV is bigger than that of one's neighbour). I am sorry but this is not true.

Latouche asks for 'de-growth', that is, for a way of living together based on sobriety. In other words: too many goods, less work. For this important French scholar a more balanced relationship between the individual and nature consists in acknowledging that development is an invention of mankind and that it is possible to return to a 'convivial' dimension. We need less 'wealth', but more 'well living'.

To sum up, the authors mentioned above tend to invert the trend and to confirm that resources are means and not purposes. The accumulation of capital results deeply distant from any orientation based on the

DOI: 10.1057/9781137467232.0002

quality of life, especially in the case of those who regulate their existence on the basis of a fixed income.

These are the stimuli provided by Donatella Padua's book, which we can consider a useful and salutary contribution to the rethinking of crystallized convictions. What remains to know is the future ahead of us. We wonder which path the capitalist system will follow at the end of the present economic crisis: The frenzy of orthodox neo-liberalism, a rapid decline towards new horizons or, more realistically, some reforms where it will be possible to sense the influence of Keynesian principles. We will see. What we know is that we currently need to regain confidence in order to create values and, no less important, we have more than ever the right to imagine a better world.

Renato Fontana
Rome, 27 July 2014

Note

Donatella Padua can be contacted at donatella.padua@unistrapg.it

DOI: 10.1057/9781137467232.0002

palgrave▶pivot

Introduction

Abstract: *Why does trust collapse during crises and when does it become, instead, a driving force of social and economic change? How may trust become a chief motive of growth recovery by building value?*

By applying the sociological components of trust to the social thought of John Maynard Keynes, Padua tackles topics as rationality and irrationality, individualism, values, government, growth and development, coordinating them with the current global issues of equality and redistribution, techno-finance and social capital. While trust impacts on the relationship between risk, uncertainty and security, the original concept 'Nominal Economy' explains the rise of the new strong powers. Under a Keynesian perspective, only focused interventions of 'Economy of Trust' may positively build value as social capital, channelling trust towards institutional bodies responsible for institutional trustworthiness.

Keywords: development; Economy of Trust; equality; irrationality; John Maynard Keynes; Nominal Economy; rationality; techno-finance; trust generates value

Padua, Donatella. *John Maynard Keynes and the Economy of Trust: The Relevance of the Keynesian Social Thought in a Global Society*. Basingstoke: Palgrave Macmillan, 2014. DOI: 10.1057/9781137467232.0003.

From the beginning of the 2007 subprime economic downturn, all trust indexes registered a substantial drop. Nonetheless, in these circumstances, never has the word 'trust' been so frequently invoked. Apparently, a relentless 'trusting trust' has been the only solution to these issues of inexperienced complexity.

To the extent of designing possible ways out, in the institutional, social and economic contexts, both at national and international level, two key questions have been raised: *Why trust in the socio-institutional-economic system collapses during crises and when it becomes, instead, a driving force of social and economic change? How trust may become a chief motive of economic growth recovery by building social value?*

Notwithstanding the complexity of these questions, the purpose of this book is to try to provide answers to these queries by applying sociology to the theories of John Maynard Keynes. Indeed, in the Keynesian assumption, the issue of trust enters effectively into the dynamics of social interactions, in connection with economic action. This view suggests a complex global scenario where the understanding of the concept of trust opens the doors to original models of interpretation of social and economic issues.

Post-modernity develops in a global context where social, economic, political, and technological systems tend to act as organic bodies, evolving and interacting with the environment (Luhmann, 1979). Given the complex interconnection of these systems, a major challenge is to grasp their dynamics: the 2007 downturn and the 'environmental' impact yielded by the current recession have indicated how the models of interpretation of reality were misleading and how the financial slump was behind a deep economic, political and social crisis.

From several sides, the need for new patterns of understanding of the global system is rising. This is based on the consideration that the global system must be regarded as a *unicum*, composed of multiple sub-systems, interconnected thanks to the growing pervasiveness of technology (Luhmann, 1979; Castells, 1996; Beck, 2000; Fukuyama, 1996; Giddens, 1994; Morin, 2001).

The high level of complexity of the processes of comprehension of socio-economic systems is motivated also by their interrelation with human behaviour: the 2007 crisis as, going back in time, the 1929 slump or the financial panic of 1893 are the result of a criss-crossing of individual irrational feelings, crowd behaviours, actions of banks and lending institutions, companies, governments – it is evident how the facts generated by this complex reality are originated by exchanges and interactions

DOI: 10.1057/9781137467232.0003

within a global context of an interconnected network of relationships. What flows within these networks are resources of various origins: money, information, but also feelings and emotional impulses driving irrational actions. Indeed, trust appears to represent the best antidote against feelings of uncertainty or fear spreading amongst people.

This age, designed by sociologists as 'reflexive modernization' (Beck et al., 1994), so discontinuous towards modernity, can just look at itself, overlapping realms which were once separated.

If the philosopher of complexity, Edgar Morin, suggests that it is necessary to embrace knowledge through an interdisciplinary approach, the Master of Sociology, Max Weber, indicates the need for a 'comprehensive' study of reality: the economy is not only driven by rationality but also by irrational actions, impulses and emotions, in other words, by the non-logic Paretian action – indeed, the economy founds itself on uncertainty. Not only has Keynes realized this concept in the history of economics, but he has also developed a 'General Theory' founded on uncertainty (Skidelsky, 1996).

Because of Keynes' ability to put together an organic and systemic vision with a pervasive sense of instability on the economic and social evolutionary processes, based on the depth of analysis of the irrational behaviour of individuals, I have allowed myself to call Keynes the 'economist of complexity'.

It is evident how this approach puts the Master in opposition to classical economists and their successors: to the monetarist attempt to harness this complexity in sophisticated econometric models, Keynes opposes the emotional essence governing irrational impulses of individuals.

After all, even the sociologist Georg Simmel, in his *The Philosophy of Money*, maintains, 'the fact that two people exchange their products is by no means simply an economic fact' (Simmel, 1987, p. 87). Economic facts cannot be isolated from other psychological, moral, aesthetic facts and no science is ever in the position to reach an exhaustive comprehension of the totality of any reality.

This is the ground on which the concept of 'Economy of Trust' nurtures, based on the complex balance between people–organizations–government. This original concept intends to design the process of value-building, grafted by trust as a replacement tool of assurance and control institutions, which proved to be particularly weak during the 2007 crisis.

DOI: 10.1057/9781137467232.0003

Trust builds on uncertainty: the more the feeling of uncertainty grows, the more people resort to it, thanks to its ability to provide certainty and reliability. The rational and irrational component of trust, so dynamic, helps to curb the action, deploys substitutive or completion roles, and decelerates or accelerates processes; if well managed, it may become an extraordinary economic, social and political tool. Unfortunately, the problem is that trust is neither manageable nor controllable in just one way; nevertheless, from the analysis of the components of the socio-logical concept of the *Economy of Trust*, some indications suitable to the identification of operational tools take shape.

Keynes was the first economist to fully comprehend the scope of the trust-lever. Even in the understanding of the difficulty to manage trust, the study of the dynamics of such a construct allowed the Master to access a new interpretation of economics: the *Animal Spirits*, namely irrational impulses, provide not only an explanation of economic cycles valid today, but also of current economic dynamics.

This volume aims to offer an interpretation of the thought of John Maynard Keynes through the sociological components of the construct of trust – rationality and irrationality, individualism, values, government, global society, growth, development, are just some of the topics tackled. Due to disciplinary competence limitations, the most technical aspects related to the Keynesian economic theory are kept out of the analysis; however, they all re-enter the game as determinants of the social thought of the economist: employment, prices, income, return on equity, produc-tion, are variables linked to the relationship between development and new poverties in terms of equality and redistribution; between democ-racy and capitalism, in terms of the relationship among techno-science, capitalistic and political economics; and between fragmentation and social cohesiveness, in relation to the concept of social capital. Within this conceptual frame, the topic of trust powerfully pervades within the fabric of the social and public life, inside national boundaries and in the global scenario, impacting on the relationship between risk, uncertainty and security. This occurs through different forms of the trust construct: 'interpersonal trust', 'institutional trust' and 'systemic trust'.

The gap between people and institutions emerging in this scenario show complex reasons upstream and puzzling consequences down-stream. In fact, institutions appear to experience difficulties in keeping promises and supporting collective projects related to the 'Trust in Development' model (Cesareo, 1990); the phase shift between the needs

DOI: 10.1057/9781137467232.0003

of governance on a global scale and the power of action within national boundaries makes political institutions powerless in satisfying their institutional tasks, as does the preservation of the democratic model, the assurance of security, the regulation of economy, the commitment to employment and creditworthiness in general. As a consequence, in the power vacuum determined by the deficiencies of the regulatory institutions in authority, trust regulates the social order (Barber, 1983) following spontaneous modes: it is the *Nominal Economy*. This second original concept introduced in this reflection extends the notion of speculation economy to social, cognitive and ethical topics tied to: irrationality; subjectivity in the creation of value; and lack of responsibility.

In the *Nominal Economy*, trust operates by complying with the needs of the 'new strong powers', as, for instance, hedge funds societies, rating agencies, financial companies. Virtual liquidity managed by these new global institutions is far away from the rules of the monetary system assured by the government and community (Simmel, 1987). Indeed, it refers to the interpersonal trust generated between salesmen (as financial brokers) and clients in banks, financial communities, markets and stock exchanges and, in general, to trust nurtured within the networks where liquidity circulates.

These trust dynamics that originated in a systemic framework – volatile and uncertain, not predictable by linear and rational logics – reinforce the irrational component of behaviour, giving origin to narratives (Bruner, 1988). Such processes appear to be at the base of the transmission of the Keynesian Animal Spirits, responsible for economic cycles.

Along with these considerations, the reflection provides indications on a possible model of economic development, the *Economy of Trust*, able to generate value through the use of the lever-confidence. It's an approach inspired from the Keynesian theory, which retains some regulatory aspects while blurring the more extreme interventionist positions.

The model is founded on the assumption that in a highly asymmetric social and economic context such as the one we are currently experiencing, institutions need new interpretive models that consider the irrational side of human actions, identified in exemplary fashion by John Maynard Keynes.

DOI: 10.1057/9781137467232.0003

1
Complexity

Abstract: *In this chapter Padua analyses the Keynesian organic interdependency within the environmental complexity of the current socio-economic system. The consequences of such a complex scenario are: inability to predict; need for a holistic vision; and causes not attributable to the effects.*

By assuming a progressive prevalence of the intangible over the tangible dimension, in opposition to the 'Real economy', Padua explains the original concept of 'Nominal economy' as a form of unregulated and unethical speculative economy operating in the complex global financial environment, generating wealth asymmetries and a tendency towards fluctuations. This opposition justifies an evolution of the meaning of value in the current economy, reflecting the dualism between the roles of goods (tangible) and reputation (intangible) in the process of building value.

Keywords: economic asymmetries; holistic and organic approach to complexity; intangible; real-nominal; reputation; speculative economy; tangible

Padua, Donatella. *John Maynard Keynes and the Economy of Trust: The Relevance of the Keynesian Social Thought in a Global Society.* Basingstoke: Palgrave Macmillan, 2014. DOI: 10.1057/9781137467232.0004.

DOI: 10.1057/9781137467232.0004

Yes, I've found a flaw. I don't know how significant or permanent it is. But I've been very distressed by that fact.

You found that your view of the world, your ideology was not right, it was not working?

Absolutely, precisely. You know, that's precisely the reason I was shocked, because I have been going for forty years or more with very considerable evidence that it was working exceptionally well.[1]

With this statement the classical economic legacy, on which the global economic élites nurtured for the past forty years, appears to be deeply compromised.

At the beginning of the third millennium, the acknowledgement of the fallacy of the sophisticated econometric models spawned by the prevalent think-tanks has led to a deep revision of the principles of the economic mainstream. Acknowledging that the dominant theories weren't able to grasp the deep shift of context taking place at a global level, a rethinking of the economic laws and their relations with social contexts turns out to be crucial. In this shift of scenario, what ought to be investigated is the meaning behind the recovery of the philosophy and thought of John Maynard Keynes.

In the early 1990s as nowadays, John Maynard Keynes is the economist in opposition to the mainstream thought. The chief enemy of the Keynesian theories is the absolute rationality, being the epistemological pillar of the classical theory and the conceptual foundation of the mainstream economic theories. Among these, the monetarist theory, entrenched in stiff and sophisticated econometric models, represents the evolution of the classical thought, rooted in the same principles as the Rational Choice Theory.[2]

During Keynes' lifetime, the dialectic verve of Keynes and his strong personality were able to effectively justify the predominance of his theses against the dominant theories; today, indeed, Keynesian thought requires a reassessment to capture the aspects of newness and provide useful interpretations in light of the current socio-economic context.

After all, The General Theory was written in 1936, in a peculiar historical circumstance, following the Great Depression of 1929. No doubt Keynes, today, would be able to propose an adequate adaptation of his theories, although necessarily going against the economic mainstream

DOI: 10.1057/9781137467232.0004

once more. Nevertheless, it wouldn't be a problem for John Maynard Keynes, as he used to state: 'Worldly wisdom teaches that it is better for the reputation to fail conventionally than to succeed unconventionally' (Keynes, 2006, p. 344).

Keynes was not conventional at all: he had a striking personality; he was an enlightened intellectual, indeed controversial, harshly criticized and beloved at the same time; a profound, discursive, asystematic and passionate intellectual, fiercely supportive of innovative thinking.

When we say Keynes' thought was against the mainstream theories, we refer also to another aspect, not of minor relevance and of pragmatic essence: scientific communities are naturally resistant to change. Any evolution of the scientific knowledge, as Kuhn maintains (Kuhn, 1962), involves long lead-times and requires the endorsement of the dominant scientific community. As a matter of fact, at its introduction, The General Theory received harsh distrust and suspicion by scientists. Only at the start of the 1930s did it succeed in becoming the new dominant economic paradigm, and remained so up to the 1960s. In those years of economic boom, the Keynesians, or the 'economists of the neo-classical synthesis', to keep the theory in vogue, tempted mediation with the classical theory. The outcome was a hybrid theory, compromising the tightness of the general theoretical framework and booting it to its decline.

Even though during the American Nixon's presidency the successful outcomes of the economic policies carried the banner of the economic Keynesian policy, during the 1970s' oil crisis its decline peaked at an all-time high. In 1976, a release by the Prime Minister of the Labour Party, James Callaghan, officially put an end to it: the expansion of public spending to exit the recession was behind excessive inflationary pressures.

That moment heralded the final collapse of the Keynesian theories that were never more taken into consideration, at least not until the dawn of the third millennium.

At the beginning of the 1929 slump Keynes was writing to his wife Lydia Lopokova: 'I'm fashionable again.'[3] Probably, today we may think that the Keynesian theories are fashionable again in a moment in which many economists appear to have suddenly turned to becoming Keynesians.

In this chapter we tackle two initial subjects allowing the connection of John Maynard Keynes' thought to the current socio-economic context: the subject of complexity and the topic of what we define in this book as

DOI: 10.1057/9781137467232.0004

the 'Nominal Economy'. These two issues drive the reflection on to the second original concept of this volume: the 'Economy of Trust'.

Keynes, the 'Economist of complexity'

> Who could ever think that to understand the mood of Wall Street we should have analysed the Italian bonds rates? (Michael Mayo, trader, in an interview with the *New York Times*[4])

This book is being written at the time of a very early recovery from a global economic downturn we could define with no antecedents. Its cause has to be traced in the financial crisis of the subprime mortgages, started in 2008. Nevertheless, even though early positive signs show evidence that the economic global growth is starting to rise (largely on account of recovery in the advanced economies), downward revisions to growth forecasts in some economies highlight continued fragilities, and downside risks remain.[5]

As a result, the recessive consequences of the 2008 financial slump left us in a phase of previously unexperienced global uncertainty. In fact, as for a domino effect starting in 2010, the crisis of credibility of the financial markets had affected the trustworthiness of the solvency of the public debt of some governments up to the point where it compromised their sovereign powers (Elliot, 2011). For this reason, although not exclusively, a crisis of credibility of the whole European region was triggered. It dealt with a crisis of liquidity and solvency; nevertheless, it was, and it is still today, in the aftermath of its peak, also a political, industrial, labour crisis and, most of all, a generalized crisis of trust.

A deep destabilization of the systemic balances has followed, involving economics, politics, society and values at a global level. The current international structure of sovereign orders owes its origin to the peace of Westphalia in 1648. Since that historical moment, the geo-political, economic and social context has shown a constant evolution.

Indeed, some 'accelerators of change' appear to have been catalysts of the process: accelerators of a historical nature, such as the fall of the bipolar world; technological, as with the growth of the digital networks; economic, such as the growth of new economic powers; political, as in the loss of dominant ideologies. This allows us to say that we are in the middle of a 'revolutionary' era: connectivity, complexity, intangibility, risk, individualization are paradigms of human action, tightly connected

DOI: 10.1057/9781137467232.0004

one to the other. The issue is that the prevalent models of understanding of reality adopted by the governing institutions and by the economic élites were *those of yesterday.*

In this framework, the meaning of the recovery of John Maynard Keynes as the thought of the 'opposition' takes shape.

John Maynard Keynes sheds light on the necessity to reset our mindsets: by encouraging us to shift from a culture of certainty to a culture of the uncertain, from calculation to intuition, from the probability to the concept of 'convention',[6] from anticipation to adaptation, from action to relation. Keynes offers us a view of the economic reality which may be sociologically interpreted as subjective and relational: the 'Animal Spirits' described in The General Theory (we will deepen the concept in Chapter 2) explain the human action according to dynamics which are illogical, instinctual, irrational, able to transmit emotions from person to person. These are the key variables behind the generation of the economic cycles. The General Theory, however, is not a Treatise about the uncertainty of expectations: it is founded *on* the uncertainty of expectations (Skidelsky, 2010).

In this frame of irrationality and uncertainty, a conceptual clarification has to be made: The General Theory, representing together with the Treatise on Money the most relevant theoretical bases of the Keynesian thought, never puts into question the capitalistic assumption. The capitalistic model has been shown to dominate up to today, as Fukuyama, indeed, maintains (Fukuyama, 1996). Furthermore, it is worth saying that the evolution of the economic-political scenario shows signs of interest even by those countries that yesterday ranked it as the number one enemy, one among all, China.

Keynes agrees with the principles of capitalism, viewing them as a founding pillar of economic thought. In opposition to the School of Frankfurt and to the 'Critical Theory' according to which capitalism, the technocratic system and economic rationality are responsible for commodifying and planning every aspect of human life, Keynes relies on the capitalistic model assigning a key role to it. The economist, however, puts it as the basis of the process of development only up to the achievement of a defined objective, and once accomplished, the capitalist principles fade towards models inspired to aesthetical philosophies aiming towards the luxury of leisure time and intellectual freedom.

What Keynes contrasts, in line with current reactions of some political and economic lobbies and most of the global civil society (phenomena such as Occupy Wall Street), instead, is the deep absence of rules

DOI: 10.1057/9781137467232.0004

characterizing the liberal model up to nowadays, relying on the self-regulating powers of the markets. It represents a condition of deregulation that
Émile Durkheim would define as anomic, as the freedom of the single
individual expresses itself without any form of social compensation.
The burst of one of the first historical financial bubbles, as the one of
1929 (following other historical speculative bubbles such as the Tulip
bubble of the first half of the seventeenth century and the one of the
South Sea Company in 1720), encouraged Keynes towards an interventionist approach by introducing the regulatory role of the government
in the stabilization of economic cycles. Nowadays, the need to get
back to some sort of order in global finance is invoked (notwithstanding all the possible political bonds and restrictions) even by a country
traditionally supportive of liberal politics such as the United States of
America.[7] However, the introduction of regulatory interventions in an
economic, political and social texture which is deeply interwoven, and
thus complex, appears as a daunting task.
All these premises stimulate a study of the Keynesian thought under
original perspectives, as the sociological perspective applied to the
Keynesian thought may provide a new interpretations to the current
socio-economic scenario. In this light, we could challenge a new definition
of Keynes as an economist precursor of the idea of a 'complex socio-economic system': indeed, his 'macro' theory, according to which the global
economy might be seen as a set of open and interdependent systems, owns
the ontological premises of the paradigm of complexity, which is, today, at
the core of social sciences: interdependency and organicity.
On this conceptual basis let's try to understand the feature of interdependency and organicity, emblematic within the complex Keynesian
macro-economics.

Environmental complexity

> The aquarium is a universe, where, as in a pond or in a natural lake, as in any
> other place of our planet, animal and vegetal creatures live together generat-
> ing a biological balance. (K. Lorenz, *The Ring of King Salomon*[8])

The etymology of the word 'complexity' origins from the Latin verb
complector (composed of: *cum-plecto*), which means to fold together, to
roll up. This verb opposes the verb *explicare* (*ex-plicare*), which means to
unfold or disclose, in the sense of 'opening'. What is 'complicated' (from

DOI: 10.1057/9781137467232.0004

the Latin *cum-plicato*) hides something, what is 'disclosed' (*ex-plicato*) is intelligible. The verb *cumprehendere* (in Latin, *cum-prehendere*), instead, means to embrace, to cum-prehend, that is, to embrace the totality of the elements altogether. This is the verb that, under a conceptual standpoint links itself more consistently to the understanding of our concept of complexity, as illustrated below.

The opposition between explanation (*Erklären*) and comprehension (*Verstehen*) is a core topic of sociology, fully addressed by Weber (Weber, 1958, p. 218). The distance between the two concepts marks a clear-cut boundary between two sociological realms: the first is rational, logical and positivistic. Through the process of the scientific experiment it succeeds in achieving the understanding of reality and in *explaining*, reconstructing it to reach knowledge; the second is the irrational one, 'comprehending' (cum-prehending) reality by embracing it in its entire expressive totality, to offer an interpretation of the emotional, irrational side of human action, not graspable by the scientific experiment. Weber maintains that knowledge might be achieved only by putting together explanation and comprehension, by embracing both the rational and irrational side of the individual, coupling a logical-mathematical process along with an interpretative approach. Also the Keynesian approach appears to understand the relevance of joining a rational analysis (econometric models) to an irrational interpretation (Animal Spirits) of the causal process at the base of the economic behaviour.

This comparison between the two scientists, Weber in sociology and Keynes in Economics, enlightens in us the need for a holistic or global model of comprehension of complexity inspired by both a rational-logic and comprehensive approach, inclusive of the emotional and illogical expression of human action.

What is complexity?

The experiment of the sand pile run by the scientist Bak, in which he constructed a conical sand pile through slowly dropping sand and observing the moment in which the conical sand pile collapses (Bak and Chen, 1991, pp. 46–53), led the scientist to formulate hypotheses on the 'Critical Structural Instability' of the sand pile cone.

Instability is such that the addition of a single sand grain may initiate an avalanche involving the whole structure of the cone, as reversely, being uninfluential on its totality.

DOI: 10.1057/9781137467232.0004

Stability is only just apparent, while the reality of facts lies within the full unpredictability of its dynamic: being impossible to understand and predict which grain of sand and in which moment it makes the cone collapse, and by using traditional scientific methods and tools it is not viable to connect a cause to its effects. Complex systems, in fact, evolve through a 'critical phase' in which a minimal interference on the balance may trigger an event of any entity.

The conclusions drawn from the Bak sand pile experiment drive us to the awareness that a complex system such as our global society cannot be explained by studying its single components separately, indeed, only a holistic and systemic vision helps to *comprehend* the whole. In fact, the single grain or the single individual cannot provide any explanation of the social context: postmodern processes of subjectivization, that is, the further differentiation of the processes of individualization of people (Touraine, 1997), do not allow us to comprehend the social order and its principles by analysing the single element. In the same way, we may maintain that the instability of financial prices and social investments is due to the unfeasibility to provide an explanation of what has occurred before and after the moment of the investment decision. Touraine argues, reversely, that it is required to start from the ability of human systems to produce norms, or what are called 'values', and to build up its functioning. Social facts are neither subjective nor objective, but relational (Touraine, 1997).

In fact, the interdependency of the parts within the system guides us towards different ways of comprehending the complex reality surrounding us.

Yet in ancient times, sophists offered an interpretation of the complexity of the world via the art of 'the variation of the viewpoint': this key process led to the identification of new solutions, overcoming the patterns of the traditional thought, apparently not efficient in the solution of problems. This reflection was strongly reinforced by the sociologists and philosophers of complexity. Edgar Morin, the eminent French sociologist, emphasizes the relevance of a global approach to knowledge (Morin, 2001), by connecting elements, that is, the specific disciplinary fields, to the totality of knowledge.

Based on similar premises, Ilya Prigogyne (Prigogyne, 1986), the Nobel Prize winner, has developed a Theory of Complexity explaining phenomena via equations able to design relationships and interactions not accessible to traditional linear mathematic models. The chemist and

DOI: 10.1057/9781137467232.0004

physicist have achieved these results through the study of entropy, a process belonging to thermodynamics explaining how the phenomenon of self-realization is a complex occurrence in nature. Prigogyne's theory succeeds in integrating traditionally incompatible viewpoints such as the humanistic culture, the culture of art and human sciences, and the realm of the scientific knowledge.

Along this pattern, an apparently distant science such as thermodynamics is adopted to explain phenomena applicable to social, economic and political contexts.

Biology, instead, is the springboard used to define the concept of complexity for Niklas Luhmann, who defines a system as a self-referent entity, in a constant self-reproducing activity and in osmosis with the environment (Maturana and Varela, 1987, p. 713).

Also Ulrich Beck, in his studies on risk (Beck, 2000, p. 35), contrasts the legitimacy of the statistical approach as the concept of 'average' overrides the uneven distribution of risk within society. Statistics, moreover, don't take into consideration the factor of human variability: Weber has explained that any discussion becomes useless if it doesn't take into consideration the social structures of power and distribution, of norms and dominant rationalities.

Indeed, the economic or social system appears to behave as an 'adaptive complex system', characterized by a heterogeneous presence of actors interacting one with the other. Through relationships, they generate an 'emerging' global system, representing something new and different against the sum of all relationships. This model of an 'emerging' system, adopted by the recent Relational Sociology (Donati, 1991), implies that it is not possible to understand the system only by observing some parts disjointedly.

Along this line of thought, John Maynard Keynes, just challenged as 'the economist of complexity' introduces the concept of a complex and 'open' system, that is, dependent on changes in other variables of linked systems. This interdependency evidenced by the Keynesian macroeconomic theory, assigns a characteristic of *organicity* to the functional relationships among the variables of the systems. The concept of organic interdependency constitutes the methodological assumption behind the harsh critique that Keynes operates towards the classical economy, firmly rooted in the hypothesis of 'independency from'. The entire General Theory grounds itself on the assumption of organic interdependency equalling an assumption of 'not independence from'. This consid-

DOI: 10.1057/9781137467232.0004

eration allows comprising The General Theory amongst the theories of complexity (Carabelli, 1991). The definition itself of 'General' Theory clearly explains that the purpose of such a title is to reject the restrictive assumption of independence, thus counterposing the classical theory's arguments and conclusions. This liability of the classical economy, defined as *ignoratio elenchi* (Keynes, 1971–89, VII, p. 259) concerns the extension of an analysis applied to a part of a system, with no changes, to a whole system (Carabelli, 1988, p. 117). This means to abstract the system from its variability, circumstance not sustainable to Keynes.

All these considerations provide the following relevant indication for the comprehension of the socio-economic context, that is, *the need to frame information and knowledge inside their context, their complexity and environment.*

Today, many financial experts follow this route. They analyse the stock exchange fluctuations and the effects of economic measures by intersecting them with the totality of the socio-political events, assumed as useful indicators of economic behaviour. The keen eye on the global vision cannot help but connect the Tahir Square 2011 events to the Euro crisis and the fluctuations of the BTP-BUND spread: if Europe, at a socio-political level, showed itself incapable of internal sympathy towards the vessels crowded with desperate immigrants in the summer of 2011, it is probable that the same attitude may be adopted in political economic behaviour towards indebted countries (Bremmer, 2007).

In view of the topics we will tackle in the discussion about the concept of Economy of Trust, it has to be evidenced that the idea of *organicity* strongly ties to the concept of *probability*, a focal point of the Keynesian theory. This is made clear in the 'Treatise of Probability', whereas probability is not based on assumptions of independence of the variables – as a matter of fact, the whole system might be altered by variations in the values of the variables, and these variations are not predictable. Indeed, within a system an effect is not traceable back to its cause with certainty (Keynes, 1971–89, VIII, pp. 276–8; Carabelli, 1988).

What does complexity imply?

Based on what was said about complexity, let's try to point out the pragmatic implications to the socio-economic realm. It ought to be noted how these inferences interestingly overlap with many assumptions of the Keynesian paradigm.

DOI: 10.1057/9781137467232.0004

Inability to predict

At the beginning of the twentieth century, when evidences of complexity were emerging, quantum physics demonstrated the infeasibility to predict both the precise position of a particle, whose motion, even in a limited portion, is random, and the dynamics of non-linear systems (the concept of linearity makes the sum of causes correspond to the sum of its effects). This science also demonstrated that two A and A^1 systems, similar at their initial states, may vary more over time (Magrassi, 2011, p. 62). This scientific evidence reinforces the idea that, in principle, making predictions is not feasible. To reinforce this concept, the reductionist approach, according to which the understanding of phenomena has to go through the study of its microscopic particles, is coming to an end: the whole techno-social system lets out a new reality from the expected behaviour of its single components. For instance, the 'wisdom of crowds' phenomenon (Surowiecki, 2004), or the bottom-up wave of protests raised on the Internet as the Arab Spring movement, is a clear demonstration of it (Magrassi, 2011 pp. 61–5). Also Keynes, through the theory of the uncertainty of expectations, confirms the impossibility to safely predict the future.

Holistic vision

Apparently, the dominant theoretical paradigm, having contributed to driving us to the current economic recession, as stated by Alan Greespan, has offered an interpretation of the economic system associated to linear models close to the cause–effect Weberian pattern. Opposed to the linear model, a 'holistic vision' might be more helpful in grasping the meaning of the current socio-economic phenomena. As a matter of fact, any simplification of the complex reality strictly related to the monetarist econometric models appears, increasingly with greater evidence, unable to represent reality. It is intuitive, for example, how the price of a bond or of a good, might influence the price of another bond or good, thus evidencing non-linearity; just as it is true that economic actors don't behave in a totally rational way. Moreover, Daniel Kahneman won a Nobel prize in Economics in 2002 by demonstrating the fallacy of the assumptions behind the rational behaviour shown during the 1970s; and Joseph Stiglitz maintains that markets are fully efficient only in extremely rare circumstances (Nobel prize for a work of 1975) and might considerably drift away from the 'equilibrium' point (Magrassi, 2011, p. 63).

DOI: 10.1057/9781137467232.0004

Keynes, as the economist of complexity, thanks to macro-economics appears to embrace a systemic and holistic vision.

Causes not traceable back to their effects

In light of all that has been said, the community of sociologists, from Zygmunt Bauman to Manuel Castells, from Ulrich Beck to Amartya Sen, appears to agree on the idea that the economic realm is intrinsically related to the social, political and institutional one. This implies that the consequences of the economic, political and social decisions at a global level are connected to issues such as development, distribution and redistribution of wealth, inequality and freedom. The common error is that, while experts try to explain phenomena, they connect effects to causes and factors which are poorly isolable. Instead, a system interlinked by highly specialized macro-realms, each interdependent to the other, corresponds to the 'absence of specific causes and isolable responsibilities' (Beck, 2000, p. 43). In other words, to go back to our Bak sand pile experiment, it is furthermore difficult to isolate that specific sand grain originating the collapse of the whole system. Beck deepens the concept by explaining that 'the highly specialized division of labour corresponds to a general abetment and this latter to a general lack of responsibility. Anyone is both cause and effect, and in this way, also not-cause' (Beck, 2000): as a result, it appears that *the systemic condition de-responsibilizes*. A concept which will appear to be useful in our further reflection.

How does an individual manage complexity? Many strategies appear to be applicable. The sociologist Luhmann (Luhmann, 1979), for example, explains that the individual has a tendency towards 'simplification' to satisfy an innate instinct for survival. This tendency is at the basis of a special kind of trust, namely defined as 'systemic trust'. This feeling comprises, among the various expressions that will be analysed throughout the volume, trusting subjects of 'proved experience'. In fact, the superiority in knowledge of these entities represents itself as a grant of reliability. This tendency is validated by the Edelman Trust Barometer,[9] a global indicator of the levels of trust, according to which the levels of credibility of academics or experts are placed at the top levels: in 2014, 67% of the individuals interviewed within the Edelman Panel declared them as being 'very/extremely credible', followed by companies' technical experts at 66%, financial or industrial analysts at 53%, and government officials or regulators at 6%.

DOI: 10.1057/9781137467232.0004

Nominal economy vs. real economy

Growth of 'nominal' economy:

Volume of OTC[10] derivatives

By end of June 2007:	516 trillion dollars (Bank for international settlements)
By end of 2008:	592 trillion dollars
By end of June 2011:	708 trillion dollars: over 10 time the world GNP.[11]

The terms used by sociologists to describe the age in which we live are varied, with each relating to a specific theory: post-modernity, after-modernity, reflective modernity. These definitions represent theoretical grounds where concepts such as global, relational, liquid and risk societies nurture. However, notwithstanding the variety of definitions, a prevalent orientation of the sociological community evidences a common feature: the progressive prevalence of the intangible over the tangible.

Such a tendency is reflected in various domains of the human action, for example: in the communicative action, by the relationship between reality and virtuality, altering real information through word-of-mouth and virtual 'buzz' on a global scale; in the domain of risk, as Beck argues, through the transformation of wealth, generating within class society tangible effects while in the case of poverty, dissolving into an intangible reality[12] (Adam et al., 2000, p. 36); or, in the domain of consumption, through a progressively dematerialized and differentiated offer focused on product-values rather than on product functionality. Other signs, although conceptually less clear-cut, are originated by the shift from the paradigm of action to the paradigm of relationship (Donati, 1991). Once more, this process shows again how its barycentre is moving from a tangible individual dimension to an intangible relational context.

These phenomena shed light on the global dynamic of the creation of value and, coherently, on the specific realm of the economy. On these grounds, they appear to translate into a symbolic shift between *real* and *nominal*.

In economics, the *nominal value* (or face value) is the stated value of an issued security. It refers to the price of a share, a bond, or a stock when it was issued, rather than its current market value.[13]

Unlike the classical Value Theory built by economists such as Adam Smith or Ricardo, or the Marginalist revolution of Jevons, Menger and Walras, Georg Simmel is the sociologist who has studied first the economic dynamics from an interactional perspective, by tying the concept of value to exchange.

DOI: 10.1057/9781137467232.0004

According to Simmel, it's the exchange that generates value: value is not a quality of the being, but it expresses the relationships of reciprocity conveyed by the exchange. In other words, the social meaning of exchange lies in this dimension of relativity: the value of an object is not grounded on its utility as the capacity to satisfy needs and desires, but to the price that we are willing to pay in terms of sacrifice, and renounce to other exchanges acts that belong to a subjective category. In summary, value is determined by the desire of people to obtain the object, not by the value of use of the good.[14] Simmel maintains that the real economic value is a determined quantity emerging by the reciprocal measurement of two desires of relative intensity (Simmel, 1987, p. 141). In the perspective of the irrational influence, Simmel approaches Keynes, putting the psychological variable as a determinant of the assessment of the exchange value. In substance, the nominal value is nothing but a bet, as no one can definitely say if, at the end of the exchange or at reimbursement, one has gained or lost; this can only be assumed in relation to assessments and projections, therefore, the nominal value is tied to the concept of a *future* time.

The *real value*, instead, is tied to definite measurement and tightly linked to an asset, to industrial production, to the actual value of the buying power of the nominal sizes with no monetary illusion,[15] and related to the real value of wages. In substance, the real value is tied to the *present*.

Also the market value of a good or a security would appear linked to the present. In fact, it is determined by the intersection of the demand and offer produced at a specific moment on the investment market[16]. However, particularly in the financial market, the demand and offer are influenced by the expectations of traders with regards to the future trends in the price of securities (it is the prediction on the future value of securities versus the time of their assessment) and by the economic contingencies. Therefore, the market value constantly varies due to the volatility generated by the dynamism of the activities of securities trading. For these reasons and given the intrinsic speculation of the financial market, we may say that we are facing a case of nominal value.

The conceptual real–nominal dichotomy has been adopted as it appears to comprehend in the most immediate way all forms of separation between speculation and real production economy, distances between stockholders and entrepreneurship, and nominal and real values of currencies or commodities. In substance, it explains the gradual shift

DOI: 10.1057/9781137467232.0004

from 'industry' to 'security' that developed within the economic sector and is reflected in the shift from the tangible to the intangible at large.

This phase shift is also reflected in the relationship between reality and the perceived realm of individuals and collectivity. It translates into the distance between the values tied to *real numbers* as, for example, values related to employment, to GNP, to trade and payments balances, to deficits and sovereign debts, and *nominal value*, built through the levels of awareness, consciousness and induced feelings of people. Moreover, these two levels appear to be separate and far removed from each other in two ways: first in *substance* – for instance, as an economic index indicating a growth counterpoised to a general negative feeling from people, thus driving them to sell (as a circumstance when, even with interest rates lower than the previous year, people tend not to ask for credit); second, in *time* – as a negative reaction from people may occur vis-à-vis data which were already negative from time. Keynes had explained this phase shift between reality and perception with the concept of 'monetary illusion'.

Today we are living a time in which this gap between real and nominal has reached extreme consequences.

There is an 'economy flowing everyday over our heads', unbeknownst to us. It stands on laws and rules different to the economy tied to the real, and it is far from the reality of the deep current recession. It deals with financial products such as derivatives: options, futures, swaps;[16] it represents a 'nominal' economy, often speculating without ethical principles, flowing along channels parallel to the ones of regulated finance and nobody appears to be able to halt it.

What appears to have worried most is a widespread absence of awareness about the behaviour of this market during the financial crisis, when, from many sides, speculative actions and serious responsibilities about the dramatic fallouts on many people's destinies were deprecated. Notwithstanding this, the 'nominal economy' kept growing, appearing not to care at all about the worries of governments and the massive domino effect on entrepreneurs and people. This speculative finance corresponds to a generation of *nominal* wealth which is disproportionate versus the real wealth of our planet: at June 2011 it has been accounted over ten times the global GNP and it doesn't show any signs of slowing down.

The concept of 'nominal economy', therefore, has been coined to the extent of distinguishing it from the notion of 'speculative finance'.

DOI: 10.1057/9781137467232.0004

This definition, in fact, derives from a sociological perspective aiming to capture the social and ethical implications of the phenomenon of splitting-up between the real economic dimension and the nominal one.

Based on these considerations and on the following reflections, we try to give an interpretation:

> The Nominal Economy is a form of not regulated speculative economy oper-ating in the global finance. It generates deep asymmetries versus the produc-tion of real wealth and goes beyond any control of responsible institutions; it is characterized by a prevalence of irrationality on rationality; it generates subjectivity in the creation of value, tendency to fluctuations and it favours irresponsibility. The Nominal Economy represents, in most cases, the not ethical side of speculative finance.

Under a sociological perspective, the 'nominal economy' distorts the perception of the real, deceives and deludes our possibilities of growth; it gathers wealth where it already spontaneously builds up and isolates within the grip of poverty the ones that are already excluded. It profusely distributes, instead, handfuls of risk to those 'who have less', securing those 'who have more', as Beck argues, following the inverse law of wealth distribution (Beck, 2000).

The fact that nobody has succeeded to halt this speculative process says a lot about the impracticality to govern (at least, as far as we know) some mechanisms of finance. This accounts for two sets of reasons: on the one side, the level of sophistication of the financial market products, introduced under the form of particularly attractive and high-yield financial packages while hiding junk bonds into Chinese boxes; on the other, the viral circulation of the final product spreads non-investment grade bonds with an expected high yield but with a high risk level; these products lead to incorrect investment assessments, thus generating a loss of control of the risk levels of a securities portfolio. It stays in the limelight of economic news, the triple A rating of subprime mortgages issued by one of the most credited rating agencies, Standard and Poor's. Reality tells us, however, that subprime mortgages were responsible for the speculative bubble which was at the root of the current systemic crisis.[17]

Going back to the difference between nominal and real, at the beginning of the twentieth century some scientists analysed this issue. Among these, the sociologist Georg Simmel observed the evolution of the economy of money towards financial capitalism, the relationship between means and ends, and the dominance of the rational calculation on spirituality. The risk of a gap between the nominal and real, under a more ideological position, was warned by Antonio Gramsci[18] in his 'Quaderni dal carcere'. He wrote of an 'ill economy' affected by a gap between ownership and entrepreneurial function, as a result of a developed capitalism.

Keynes shows us that speculation has always been present within the stock market, as expressed by the distance between the saver and the investor. However, if in ancient and modern ages the two positions overlapped, as it was the farmer to reinvest the harvest, today, with the financialization of economy, Nominal Economy is characterized by an extremely wide gap between the saver (issuer of the security) and the owner of the security (investor).

Simmel explains that, in substance, we are progressively taking distances from 'real bases' as decisional references and evaluations moreover rely on trust mechanisms, justified by a substantial presence of irrational decisions. The sociologist sheds light on this concept, representing the various economic steps of the exchange through a teleological series of acts named 'economic series of ends'. Comparing money to securities, Simmel maintains that 'mere payment in ready cash suggests something pretty bourgeois to this businessman, since in this instance the stages of the economic series are anxiously compressed, whereas credit creates a distance between them that he controls on the basis of trust' (Simmel, 1987, p. 675).

This process leads to some consequences:

1   **Subjectivity in the definition of value**: to understand the shift of the various forms of credit from objectivity to subjectivity, it is useful to make a comparison under a socio-economic perspective between the function of cash and debt securities. This comparison is allowed thanks to the nature of liquidity of most financial products, specifically, those prevalently tied to highly speculative markets. Moreover, it is justified by the prominence of the total financial value of securities handled within the Nominal Economy, which, as we have seen, appears to be extraordinarily greater versus the correspondent regulated economy or the real economy.

Georg Simmel clarifies the concept of objectification of value which favours the circulation of money on shared trust bases: in the money economy, at each stage, coin keeps its value in relation to its nominal

DOI: 10.1057/9781137467232.0004

value.[19] Simmel argues that this confidence is granted by the issuing government *in primis* and by the economic community, ensuring that the value given in exchange for an interim value, a coin, will be replaced without loss. In this way, money objectifies, determining a condition of 'unconditioned truth' making the security an objective, exchangeable value, independent of the personal evaluation of the creditworthiness of the debtor. State and community transform into actual, tangible references, to ensure the stability of value. The same pattern is evidenced in the extension of trust from the person-to-person relationship to the government–public relationship. Simmel maintains that money is probably the highest form of trust in the State and social order.

This occurs in the money market. But in the securities economy, value loses its objectivity. To clarify the concept, if in the real economy I own ten euros and I can buy ten newspapers as I know they cost one euro each; on the other hand, in the financial economy, it is not assured that with a security of a ten euro nominal value I may buy ten other securities with a value of one euro, as I don't have any certainty that at the moment I buy them they will be worth one euro. As a matter of fact, this value is subject to the constant fluctuations determined by the supply–demand market. This dynamic sheds light on how in the securities markets, at each trading, the 'margin credit' is subject to variation (Akerlof and Shiller, 2009, p. 96) and the value of the security constantly fluctuates.

Keynes further explains that this dynamic is influenced by subjective evaluations, founded on expectations based on probability forecasts. Indeed, these estimates are calculated based on the assumption that '…, in effect, … the existing market valuation, however arrived at, is uniquely correct in relation to our existing knowledge of the facts which will influence the yield of the investment, and that it will only change in proportion to changes in this knowledge' (Keynes 2006, p. 338). This is a relevant concept of the Keynesian theory tackling the issue of decision-making behaviour and business psychology. In relation to some philosophical main beliefs described in the 'Treatise on Probability', it is tied to a key assumption of the Keynesian Theory: the principle of 'convention'.[20] Basically, Keynes explains how the community of security holders and of financial officers, consultants and other operators build their own shared reality upon which decisions are taken. It does not deal with an actual reality, as the convention's value is built on the reality *of the security*. Notwithstanding, it is perceived as *the reality* by people being linked to the *accessible* information owned by them. By way of confirmation, in

DOI: 10.1057/9781137467232.0004

Chapter 3 where we will tackle the notion of 'Trust Economy', it will become clearer how Keynes doesn't trust 'perfect information'.

As we have seen, according to Simmel, in the money market the value of the 'Simmelian coin' was granted by the central institution; In the Nominal Economy, the calculation of the increase in value of securities is founded on a subjective process: the 'nominal' economy changes the concept of value, moving it from a calculus on a real figure to a subjective evaluation based on perception, instinct, irrationality, partial information. Moreover, it dissolves those guarantee mechanisms that grant stability to value: to Keynes, the only guarantee is an 'illusion' of stability in time, produced by the community of financial analysts.

2   **Fluctuations**: in a nominal, systemic and complex economy, the role of psychology is key in influencing fluctuations. The public behaviour induced by the systemic structure, in fact, mainly subject to irrationality, determines the phases of euphoria or panic.

Keynes argues that day-to-day fluctuations in the yields of current investments, nowadays reinforced by the high speed of technological trading, '... tend to have an altogether excessive, and even an absurd, influence on the market.' (Keynes, 2006, p. 340). Even mortgage markets, now 'sublimated' in volatile securities as common stocks, are subject to cycles: a classic example is the 'subprime crisis'. Even though we will tackle the subject in a deeper way in the next chapter, in this context it is worth highlighting that among all the reasons placed at the social roots of past crises and the current recession there is the *collective behaviour*.

General common behaviour has a tendency to create stories shared by the collectivity that, once generated, tend to gain strength by spreading widely throughout crowds and triggering a self-generational process. Akerlof and Shiller explain that a 'confidence multiplier' is behind this process (Akerlof and Shiller, 2009, p. 213). History shows how the same pattern of speculative bubbles is reproduced when following this course: when scarcity of a commodity occurs, the general belief is that prices will rise; in effect, because of the rising wave of purchases, prices rise, reinforcing, in time, the common belief and the opportunity: the process, entailed by narrations, involves trust, equity, corruption and money illusion.

This dynamic is typical of nominal or speculative economy, justified by the lack of perfect information.

The elusiveness of the decision-making basis determines also an additional effect on the *reputation* of an institution, a country or a

DOI: 10.1057/9781137467232.0004

security: what is publicly being said or thought about an institution, company, country or security resist to what they are *in reality*. Reputation turns out to be a key decision-making basis of the Nominal Economy, in contrast to the trade economy of tangible, physical commodities and manufactured goods, whose quantitative dimension becomes the foundation of the calculation of estimates in the real economy (Figure 1.1).

Reputation, tied to credibility, trust, emotions, driving the synthetic transmission of a judgement, of an idea, shows a peculiar feature: it is faster than the circulation of money and much faster in respect of any exchange of goods. As a matter of fact, reputation is an intangible good transmitted by mechanisms of virality; it anticipates decisions and plays a key role in expectations and forecasts.

Therefore, reputation stands for credibility in the present and states the level of reliability. By depending on the judgement of stakeholders and crowds, being ephemeral as tied to contingency, it appears to be extremely variable; borrowing an adjective by Zygmunt Bauman, we wouldn't hesitate to call it 'liquid' (Bauman, 2002).

Reputation is a structural component of rating, being a variable integrated into the evaluation process of the reliability of the investment. The nature of the two concepts of reputation and reliability overlaps: that is, being able to transform in reality what is nominal or, based on

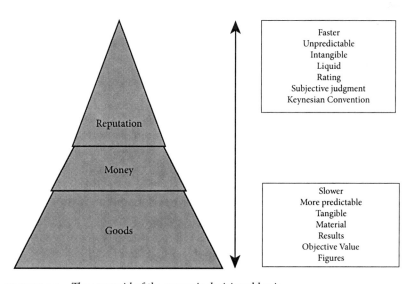

FIGURE 1.1   *The pyramid of the conomic decisional basis*

DOI: 10.1057/9781137467232.0004

a bet, by offering a measurability of a future projection. In substance, the rating is nothing but an expression of the mathematical calculation of a probability and, as such, would be rejected by Keynes. Nothing would be more unacceptable to Keynes than to give certainty to what is uncertain. Even if Keynes recognized the relevance of the mathematization of administrative procedures (Keynes gave birth to public accounting), he had always excluded the safety of the classicals' mathematical probability. Finally, taking everything into account, reputation, being a nominal market component of the economic decision-making basis, is characterized by subjectivity as its value is traced back to the perceptive dimension of the individual. Coherently, it is tied to the notion of the Keynesian convention being dependent on imperfect, limited information and based on the collective sharing of a value judgement.

In opposition, instead, goods (Figure 1.1) are intrinsically material and tangible; therefore, they follow a slower process of exchange and are more predictable in the definition of their value in relation to results in production, distribution and sales, based on actual figures.

We might say that if reputation is determined by a subjective judgement, goods define their value in relation to an 'objective' credit of their results. Yet opposed to reputation, the economic decisional basis of goods is founded on the objectivity of real figures.

Money positions itself in between reputation and goods, as getting closer to one end or the other depends on its form: from 'solid', as in cash, to 'liquid', as in OTC security.[21] In the 'liquid' form, the value of money will replicate the same behavioural pattern *of reputation* rather than of goods. That is, by progressively getting closer to volatility, its structure of value will be gradually characterized by a more irrational, subjective, nominal component, and vice-versa.

3   **Uncertainty and risk**: The sociologist Ulrich Beck, argues that the invisible cannot compete with the visible: the paradox lies in the fact that just for this reason, in the end, risks are the winners. The reason is that the propensity to ignore not perceivable, although apparently and urgently evident risks is always justified. This is the political and cultural ground on which risks and hazards nurture, grow and strengthen (Beck, 2000, p. 59).

In conditions of high fluctuation, Keynes advises that the only risk run by an investor 'is that of a genuine change in the news over the near future' (Keynes, 2006, p. 339). However, even this occurrence will be

DOI: 10.1057/9781137467232.0004

subject to a judgement on the probability that it will happen. In a situation of constancy of the 'convention', safety ties to 'short periods' and to a succession in the sequence of them. In this way, 'Investments which are "fixed" for the community are thus made "liquid" for the individual' (Keynes, 2006).

This actually generates a state of precariousness, being at the basis of the actual issue of ensuring an adequate investment.

To Keynes, factors triggering this uncertainty are, *in primis*, an increase of the stocks in the hands of those not managing the enterprise and 'not having a clue of present and future conditions of the enterprise itself' (Keynes, 2006, p. 340): in the Nominal Economy, the effective knowledge in the evaluation of the investments made by the investors or by the ones willing to buy them has seriously decreased;[22] secondly, with not a logical tie with future yields, fluctuations influence the 'conventional valuation'. In fact, Keynes argues that: 'A conventional valuation which is established as the outcome of the mass psychology of a large number of ignorant individuals is liable to change violently as the result of a sudden fluctuation of opinion due to factors which do not really make much difference to the prospective yield' (Keynes, 2006, p. 340).

It lacks a strong rooting of beliefs, says Keynes; a solid rooting in the real economy, we could add. 'The market will be subject to waves of optimistic and pessimistic sentiment, which are unreasoning and yet in a sense legitimate where no solid basis exists for a reasonable calculation' (Keynes, 2006).

4 **Lack of responsibility**: The topic of the lack of responsibility has been already tackled above by highlighting those systemic conditions in which it is not possible to connect an effect to its cause. Also the distance between the issuer (knowing the *real* value of the security) and the owner (the one valuing the security in relation not to the real value, but to the *nominal* or market value), which may be so wide as to hide the real players of global finance, determines a loss of responsibility on the real value of the security, which is subject to alteration at each act of exchange (sell or buy). We may imagine, by simplifying a series of buy-and-sell exchanges of securities, the sequence of which may be represented altogether as a 'chain', whose extremities (the initial issuer of the security on the one side and the last owner on the other) are far the one to the other and can't see each other; instead, the single rings of the chain,

DOI: 10.1057/9781137467232.0004

representing the relationship between dealer and customer, are connected one to the other.

This probably creative picture highlights indeed a relevant circumstance: the responsibility of the whole process (the chain) is segmented into the multiplicity of different relationship between each couple of players (dealer and customer). Indeed, every link in the chain is apart from all upstream and downstream stages (other chain links) and only connected relationally to the links immediately above and below. This fragmentation of relationships allows an 'institutionalized' (that is, justified and commonly taken as a shared rule) loss of responsibility motivated by the impossibility of getting to know the effective value of the relationship in *real* terms. For instance, financial products such as OTCs are often marketed with 'attractive' packaging, promising high yields. However, as said previously, being structured like Chinese boxes, they might hide junk bonds, just as the securitization of mortgages has generated, before the crisis, monkey business, opening the doors to 'organized cheating'. These are sorts of tacit agreements easily breeding within 'groups' or restricted élites where the corruption of ethical principles is fed by money greediness.

The absence of an institution in charge and in the position of offering guarantees, as it occurs in the economy of money (the State, granting for the face value), leads to a general loss of responsibility on the ethical and social compensation side. This may trigger very serious consequences: if along the articulated and extremely long chain dynamic of securities exchanges, for epidemiological reasons, the credit margin starts to grow excessively, following a snowball effect, a bubble builds up, and sooner or later it will burst.

In conclusion to this chapter we may draw some final considerations.

First, by comparing the 1929 crisis to the 2008–11 crisis, undeniable common characteristics emerge. These are traceable to the mechanics of the speculation bubble, that is, to the growth of the initial demand, followed by the bull phase of the market and the further burst of the bubble. Among the differences, instead undeniably tied to different historical times, with dissimilar political, social and economic occurrences, two aspects are worth being highlighted: the first concerns the global scale of the 2008 crisis, reaching never topped heights because of the systemic dimension. As a matter of fact, such a complex connectivity has made the individuation and prioritization of its causes an impossible task.

DOI: 10.1057/9781137467232.0004

Second, behind this recession, some 'structural' causes that during the 1929 crisis were probably just *in nuce* (in the embryonic phase) appear evident.

A reason for this is traceable to the fact that the welfare state behind the social contract has been replaced by the access to credit (Skidelsky, 2010). In other words, the citizen debt load has progressively replaced the role of protection and guarantee covered by the welfare state. What has happened in the United States with the subprime mortgages is a case in point: in a country culturally favouring and justifying indebtedness, the growth of expenditure for consumption has required continued loans to overcome the limits imposed by the immediate chargeability, thus generating progressive contractions of the savings rates; continued loan applications have raised the prices of securities and determined growing indexes of debt in the debt/revenue ratios; as a consequence, at a certain point, the system didn't support this bubble and collapsed, just like the Bak's sand pile. The policy of the global corporates has exacerbated the process, transforming it into a financial crash (Palley, 2009, pp. 14, 16).

The absence of rules in some philosophies, and with liberal strategies of economic politics not posing any form of embankment, making themselves responsible for the consolidation of some financial markets belonging to the Nominal Economy, is raising in many constituencies, the longing towards a closer gap between the nominal and real value. Someone even hopes for the return of laws such as the Glass-Steagall of 1933 that, based on different regulations, ruled out the productive economy from the speculation economy (Tremonti, 2012, p. 166).

At the end, if the growing global complexity puts us in front of connected and dynamic scenarios, where technology makes the picture even more complex, it is an almost inviable task to grasp the functioning of the economy. This means that understanding the economy (in the above mentioned sense of comprehending, from the Latin *cum-prehendere*), calls for taking into strong consideration the Keynesian 'Animal Spirits'.

Notes

1   This is an excerpt from the hearing of Alan Greenspan and Government Reform Committee Chairman Henry Waxman, California Democrat on Capitol Hill. For years, a Congressional hearing with Alan Greenspan was

DOI: 10.1057/9781137467232.0004

a marquee event. Lawmakers doted on him as an economic sage. Markets jumped up or down depending on what he said. Politicians in both parties wanted the maestro on their side. But on Thursday, 23 October 2008, almost three years after stepping down as chairman of the Federal Reserve, a humbled Mr Greenspan admitted that he had put too much faith in the self-correcting power of free markets and had failed to anticipate the self-destructive power of wanton mortgage lending. (Irwin and Paley, 2008)

2   The Rational Choice Theory was born within the nineteenth century economic thought of Adam Smith, David Ricardo, and Carl Menger, when, following the hedonistic and utilitarian theories, economists began to consider individual decision-making based on the desire to obtain reward, or fear of incurring a penalty. Rational choice theory uses a specific and narrower definition of 'rationality' simply to mean that an individual acts *as if* balancing costs against benefits to arrive at action that maximizes personal advantage.

3   On 24 October 1929 the Wall Street slump has its all-time peak. The day after, Keynes writes to his wife Lydia Lopokova, stating that he is in a 'thoroughly financial and disgusting state of mind all day' (Keynes, 1971–89, XX, p. I

4   Farina, 2011.

5   IMF, International Monetary Fund, WEO (World Economic Outlook), 2014. Available at http://www.imf.org, accessed 5 June 2014.

6   The Keynesian convention is the mode of formulation of probabilities based on the average expectations perceivable by the individual. We will deepen the concept later on in this chapter, in the section 'Nominal vs. real'.

7   Release of Paul Volker, chairman of the Economic Recovery Advisory Board under President Barack Obama from February 2009 until January 2011. Available at http://www.whitehouse.gov, accessed 6 June 2014.

8   Lorenz, 1992.

9   The Edelman Trust Barometer is an annual survey involving 27 countries and 33.000 respondents. http://www.edelman.com/insights, accessed 6 June 2014.

10   Over-The-Counter (OTC) refers to derivatives exchanged in a non regulated market.

11   Bank for International Settlements (BIS), Monetary and Economic Department, surveys on positions in global Over-The-Counter (OTC) derivatives markets: issues November 2007, May 2009, June 2008. Available at www.bis.org, accessed 25 June 2014.

12   Beck argues that modern risks are qualitatively different from earlier scarcity because the visible, tangible and localized nature of wealth can insulate the wealthy from the misfortune of the poor, while even those in relatively advantageous 'social risk positions' cannot be insulated from the intangible and deterritorialized (globalized) nature of contemporary risks such as pollution and general environmental deterioration (Adam et al., 2000).

13 Oxford Dictionary at: oxforddictionaries.com. Accessed 8 May 2014.

14 Simmel explains that:
The fact of economic exchange, therefore, frees the objects from their bond-age to the mere subjectivity of the subjects and allows them to determine them reciprocally, by investing the economic function in them. The object acquires its practical value not only by being in demand itself but through the demand for another object. Value is determined not by the relation to the demanding subject, but by the fact that this relation depends on the cost of a sacrifice that, for the other party, appears as a value to be enjoyed while the object itself appears as a sacrifice. Thus objects balance each other and value appears in a very specific way as an objective, inherent quality. (Simmel 1987, p. 77)

15 The phenomenon of the monetary illusion refers to the perception of a buying power higher versus the real, effective possibilities offered by the money owned.

16 Traditionally, swaps are the exchange of one security for another to change the maturity (bonds), quality of issues (stocks or bonds), or because investment objectives have changed. Recently, swaps have grown to include currency swaps and interest rate swaps. Derivatives are securities whose price is dependent upon or derived from one or more underlying assets. The derivative itself is merely a contract between two or more parties. Its value is determined by fluctuations in the underlying asset. The most common underlying assets include stocks, bonds, commodities, currencies, interest rates and market indexes. Most derivatives are characterized by high leverage. Available at: http://www.investopedia.com, accessed 6 June 2014.

17 The USA Department of Justice has opened an enquiry on mortgages securities, AAA rated by Standard & Poor's just before the slump. They had shown to be junk bonds, triggering the financial downturn and transforming it into a global economic crisis. A mortgages security is a type of asset-backed security that is secured by a mortgage, or more commonly a collection ('pool') of sometimes hundreds of mortgages. The mortgages are sold to a group of individuals (a government agency or investment bank) that 'securitizes', or packages the loans together into a security that can be sold to investors. Available at http://en.wikipedia.org, accessed 6 June 2014.

18 Antonio Gramsci was a communist Italian politician and thinker of the first half of the twentieth century. For his ideas, he was condemned to twenty years of prison. There he wrote the well-known work 'Quaderni dal carcere'.

19 'There has thus been established a mode of bargaining at the peak of the money economy which lightens the burden of responsibility for both parties but transposes the subjective basis of the transaction into an objective one and alleviates the disadvantage of one party at the expense of the other. Credit transactions exhibit an exact parallel to this' (Simmel, 1987, p. 425).

DOI: 10.1057/9781137467232.0004

'Although the individual buys because he values and wants to consume an object, his demand is expressed effectively only by an object in exchange. Thus the subjective process, in which differentiation and the growing tension between function and content create the object as a "value", changes to an objective, supra-personal relationship between objects' (Simmel, 1987, p. 121).

20   'The essence of this convention – though it does not, of course, work out quite so simply – lies in assuming that the existing state of affairs will continue indefinitely, except insofar as we have specific reasons to expect a change. This does not mean that we really believe that the existing state of affairs will continue indefinitely' (Keynes, 2006, p. 84).

21   'Unlike exchanges, OTC markets have never been a "place". They are less formal, although often well-organized, networks of trading relationships centred on one or more dealers. Dealers act as market makers by quoting prices at which they will sell (ask or offer) or buy (bid) to other dealers and to their clients or customers' (https://www.imf.org, accessed 21 May 2014.

22   In former times, when enterprises were mainly owned by those who undertook them or by their friends and associates, investment depended on a sufficient supply of individuals of sanguine temperament and constructive impulses who embarked on business as a way of life, not really relying on a precise calculation of prospective profit. The affair was partly a lottery, though with the ultimate result largely governed by whether the abilities and character of the managers were above or below the average. Some would fail and some would succeed. But even after the event no one would know whether the average results in terms of the sums invested had exceeded, equaled or fallen short of the prevailing rate of interest; though, if we exclude the exploitation of natural resources and monopolies, it is probable that the actual average results of investments, even during periods of progress and prosperity, have disappointed the hopes which prompted them.

Business men play a mixed game of skill and chance, the average results of which to the players are not known by those who take a hand. If human nature felt no temptation to take a chance, no satisfaction (profit apart) in constructing a factory, a railway, a mine or a farm, there might not be much investment merely as a result of cold calculation. (Keynes, 2006, p. 84)

DOI: 10.1057/9781137467232.0004

2
Trust

Abstract: *Starting with the difference between economic classical rationality and Keynesian irrationality, Padua tackles the issue of trust, analysing the five 'trust beliefs' and the concepts of institutional, systemic and interpersonal trust in relation to the irrational dynamics of the Animal Spirits. Between the constructs of trust and confidence, 'rational trust' becomes a calculation of probabilities linked to the notion of Keynesian expectations, conventional evaluation and unemployment. In this framework, the role of emotions is investigated within the perspective of the theories of 'Behavioural Economics'. An analysis of how 'trust in social systems' has worked during the 2008 financial crisis is carried out and closes the chapter, with references to the social aspects of financial networks and the role of technology within the socio-financial network.*

Keywords: institutional; interpersonal trust; Keynesian convention; rationality–irrationality; systemic; trust and confidence

Padua, Donatella. *John Maynard Keynes and the Economy of Trust: The Relevance of the Keynesian Social Thought in a Global Society*. Basingstoke: Palgrave Macmillan, 2014. DOI: 10.1057/9781137467232.0005.

Even apart from the instability due to speculation, there is the instability due to the characteristic of human nature that a large proportion of our positive activities depend on spontaneous optimism rather than on a mathematical expectation, whether moral or hedonistic or economic.

– *John Maynard Keynes, 1936*[1]

Classical rationality and Keynesian irrationality

Milton Friedman, Robert Lucas and Thomas Sargent are some of the most intransigent anti-Keynesians. Rejecting any government intervention which would halt the free functioning of a self-regulating economic market, these economists supporting the monetarist mainstream[2] advocate an economic policy active on the offer side to stimulate the economic incentive, an extreme deregulation of the goods and labour markets and the privatization of public industries. As we have mentioned in Chapter 1, the Rational Choice Theory lies at the basis of this economic theory, along which agents rationally use all available information to make their decisions. Predictions are formulated on the assumptions of the quantitative theory of money.

In Keynes' theory, instead, the behaviour of the economic actors is unlikely to be predictable: they act along a prevailing irrational drive, originated by instinctual impulses, explained by the Animal Spirits. Such behaviour, driving investment dynamics, is considered by some scholars as a form of 'weak rationality'; other scientists consider it as 'irrational': in both cases the Keynesian theory wipes out the predominance of classical rationality. His rare depth of investigation and intellectual brightness lead Keynes to become the first economist to offer an interpretation of economics based on the assumption of uncertainty, questioning the principles of rationality (Skidelsky, 1996, p. 151). Keynes highlights a substantial difference between the notion of risk and that of uncertainty: risk occurs when probabilities are known, and are, accordingly, measurable; uncertainty, instead, generates when probabilities are not known; therefore, risk stands for a subjective calculation, related to human action and to the probability distribution of results (Ormerod, 2005); a condition of uncertainty, instead, states how persons, organizations, institutions, in different

DOI: 10.1057/9781137467232.0005

circumstances, are not in the position to connect facts to possible related solutions. Due to this pervasive condition of uncertainty, economic actors can't carry out investment forecasts according to the theoretical principles of the rational choice: they may just comply with the 'conventional' probability (see Chapter 1 on Organic interdependency, p.16), which acts on the economic system as a stabilizer of investments.

The gap between the Keynesian position, founded on uncertainty, and the classical theories entails harsh critics by monetarists. Let us see on which bases.

The classical stance

To grasp the philosophy on which the classical thought is rooted we ought to go back to Adam Smith's theory and to his two masterpieces 'An Inquiry into the Nature and Causes of the Wealth of Nations' and 'Theory of Moral Sentiments'. The dilemma studied by Smith is the relationship between the self-centred individual action and the social outcome of the economic action. Basically, the crucial issue tackled by the philosopher is the following: can rationality effectively help to reach a better society?

Adam Smith in his 'Wealth of Nations' (Smith, 2010, p. 49), provides an answer to this question with an argument known to history as the 'Theory of unintended consequences', which, in turn, includes the concept of the 'Invisible Hand'. Of Smith's assumptions, two are key: first, a highly sceptical stance about the fact that individual preferences aren't rationally and purposely connected to socially-oriented choices; second, a deep distrust of the morality of wealthy people, arguing that they accomplish their insatiable desires mainly thanks to a natural selfishness and greed. There is an objection, though, to this latter observation: according to Smith, when we want to reach an objective, we obtain, at the same time, 'unwanted consequences'. This allows, unintentionally, other individuals to obtain advantages by a rational action, which stems from a rational intent. For this reason, the economist and philosopher maintains that selfish and greedy persons are guided by an 'invisible hand' allowing them to make society evolve positively, with no direct intention.

This mechanism of the Invisible Hand, conveyor of the unintended consequences, lies at the basis of the classical thought that we are going to briefly outline.

DOI: 10.1057/9781137467232.0005

Pre-Keynesian theory

When The General Theory was published in 1936, it came out during the flow of the pre-Keynesian economic era. The classic economists (the pre-Keynesians), inspired by Adam Smith's invisible hand, believed that markets, when left with no interferences, would ensure full employment by a cross benefit exchange between employer and employee. This pattern is justified by the fact that if a worker works at a lower wage than the value produced by herself or himself, the employer will profit from the margin. In this frame, unemployment is generated by those workers rejecting job offers because they believe the wage is too low for that work. This kind of unemployment is defined as 'voluntary unemployment'. Such a market economy model would lead to a balanced budget and a dramatic reduction in government control. In fact liberal capitalism is considered perfectly stable in the absence of any government intervention.

It is worth reminding ourselves that in 1936, however, with different approaches other economic and policy models were diffused with the same aim of controlling the levels of unemployment generated by the big slump of the 1930s: socialism, for instance, assigned to government a key role to replace entrepreneurships by cutting out unemployment via hiring workers directly.

The discussion on the rationality or irrationality of economic behaviour is still alive today and it shows no signs of ending. It is true, anyway, that among these dichotomic positions, reality indicates a definitely more complex scenario where rational behaviours coexist and harmonize with social attitudes. Moreover, it is necessary for such an extreme individualistic rationality (reflected in sociology via the extremist positions of the methodological individualism of Raymond Boudon or Friedrich Von Hayek) to cope with group or collective dynamics, thus more realistically reflecting the landscape in which financial exchanges take place. In this context we cannot forget the Theory of Games, according to which individuals' decisions depend on other individuals' actions within the same group and are not based on an autonomous decision. The Theory of Games, epitomized in the 'prisoner dilemma' communication plays a key role on the individuals' decisions. When it lacks, information is missing.[3]

Indeed, in the financial markets many cases occur where the lack of information affects forecasts and reflects on the provisional cross of demand and offer.

DOI: 10.1057/9781137467232.0005

The challenging of the rational paradigm through the introduction of a social variable, intrinsically cooperative, stems by the subjective side of human action. Simmel brilliantly introduced this concept in sociology, as did Keynes in economics.

Keynes' stance

We have already highlighted how Keynes' thought contrasts with the economic rationalist theories and how, nowadays, the Keynesian theory tends to be rehabilitated in order to provide an interpretation of economy along the lines of irrational assumptions. Along this line of thought, Keynes contends that Adam Smith's argument on individuals' rational behaviour in economic decision-making does not take into account drives of non-economic nature close to the non-logical Paretian actions.[4]

In a climate of uncertainty, typical of a circumstance of limited information, Keynes maintains that decisions haven't any fully rational base, as they appear to be more closely associated to 'gambling' (Keynes, 1971–89 p. 336). This behaviour is the result of vital impulses: The Animal Spirits. The Animal Spirits[5] are the result of a spontaneous stimulus to action and not, as the rational theory assumes, the outcome of a decision built on a weighted average of quantitative advantages, multiplied by quantitative probabilities (Keynes, 1973, pp. 335–6, 348).

The term 'Animal Spirits', that goes back to the Roman age and often been recalled later during the Middle Ages and the seventeenth century, gets its etymology from the Latin 'spiritus animalis': the adjective 'animal', standing as 'relative to the mind', or ' the one that gives life' (Akerlof and Shiller, 2009, p. 19) refers to an energy of mind, a basic vital drive – the animal component brings action back to the primitive and instinctual stage.

During the Roman Age it was believed that there were three spirits: the *spiritus vitalis*, having origin in the heart, the *spiritus naturalis*, in the liver, and the *spiritus animalis* in the brain. According to the philosopher George Santayana (Santayana, 1955, p. 245), the animal faith contains a subtle cognitive energy, the essence of which is 'intuition'. Nowadays, the term, evolving from its original meaning, while keeping its essence, is tied to our peculiar relationship with ambiguity or lack of guarantees.

The level of uncertainty has a relevant influence on the social fabric, shifting, over time, in general feelings of mistrust, envy, resentment and illusions. These are elements considered by behavioural economists as a significant basis of the current economic recession.

DOI: 10.1057/9781137467232.0005

Indeed, along the process of economic growth, a meaningful role is attributed to the Animal Spirits: they lie at the origin of the spirit of entrepreneurship, namely, the economic initiative which doesn't stem from calculations of future benefits, anyway, not feasible in the absence of a basis of calculation (Keynes, 2006, p. 349); it, instead, comes out of vital and trustworthy impulses.

The mathematical forecast, in substance, appears to stifle the initiative.

The Animal Spirits play a key role within social affluence: Keynes argues that 'It is safe to say that enterprise which depends on hopes stretching into the future benefits the community as a whole' (Keynes, 2006, p. 348). If, therefore, Adam Smith relates economic activity to social welfare and balance through the 'unintentionality of action', Keynes connects the two concepts by the push towards initiative, driven by the inseparable part of the Animal Spirit that instils that optimism or 'recklessness', putting distances with the thought of an ultimate loss. 'as a healthy man puts aside the expectation of death' (2006, p. 348), irrationality and optimism towards the future can't but bring advantages to the community. From the financial slump of 1929 to the oil shock of 1973, and from the stock crisis of the Black Monday of 1987 to the New Economy bubble of 2001, we have already experienced from the consequences of the various financial crisis of the twentieth century, in which proportion a collapse of the 'spontaneous optimism' (Keynes, 2006, p. 348) affects the political and social climate.

In fact, it is our instinct linked to an innate impulse towards a specific behaviour, triggered by environmental stimula that keeps the economic mechanism and the social exchange active: the choice between best alternatives provided by the environment more often follows whim and instinct, rather than calculus.

The Animal Spirits, therefore, appear to originate economic fluctuations and 'voluntary unemployment' that, as seen before, concerns those workers who are not prepared to take on a lower paying job while they look for a better paying position. This is another key aspect positioning Keynes in a stance antithetical to the classical rationality: Adam Smith's theory, in fact, is not able to explain the strong fluctuations in the economy (Smith, 1995, p. 18). Keynes, instead, not only identifies its origin in the Animal Spirits but also specifies that such a cause varies over time and according to the social and cultural contexts: as a matter of fact, mental patterns differ over time; the social fabric changes; the level of reciprocal trust alters; and the attitude towards sacrifice evolves.

DOI: 10.1057/9781137467232.0005

The notion of fluctuation, at the core of the Keynesian economic theory, may be deepened through the sociological concept of social interaction that, in turn, constitutes the epistemological foundation of the network paradigm (Simmel, 1987). Many theoretical contributions explain the concept of network: from the concept of Simmelian interaction, conceived as a reciprocal and shared individual action; the doctrine of the 'inter-human relations' founded on the social process of Leopold Von Wiese and the relational theory of Pierpaolo Donati; to the studies of Randall Collins and John Scott rooted in the Gestalt Theory and the structural-functionalist anthropology.[6] These theories explain the network as a representation of society: it appears to be formed of formed of a set of interdependent systems active in specific social landscapes, where social relations, being constitutive elements of the network, become a metaphor of belonging to complex societies and pivot of identity building.

Inside these processes, fluctuation, as a materialization of social energies beyond the single individual's action (think about word of mouth, or buzz, or panic phenomena), shows up as a transmission impulse of behaviour within the network.

To the circumstance of the speculative financial bubble, we may attribute the logic of collective irrational behaviour.[7] To better comprehend the dynamic, we may try to compare this impulse to sea waves: with a higher or lower levels of fluctuation, each water atom attracts the other to itself and makes the volume of the mass move, creating peaks and valleys, all inseparably connected in their swinging. This analogy, resembling the concept of the Paretian system,[8] alternates without any ratios or fixed relationships or rules, in constant mutation, from spikes of euphoria to troughs or panic dips. To these fluctuations there are corresponding moments of high or low trust; purchases or sales; employment or unemployment; sudden price increases or dips; appreciated or depreciated currency; gold slumps or dramatic increases; rises or decreases in estates prices – the swinging of which is materialized by stock exchange results. Collective movements, in synthesis, represent sociological explanations that shed light on mass behaviours resulting from crisis or alteration of the systemic balance.

This scenario justifies the regulatory function of the government. Keynes expects that 'the State, which is in a position to calculate the marginal efficiency of capital-goods on long views and on the basis of the general social advantage, [takes] an ever greater responsibility for

DOI: 10.1057/9781137467232.0005

directly organising investment' (Keynes, 2006, p. 350). Within a new vision of the economy, and a new role for the Government, *deficit spending*[9] became the economic tool used to overcome the Great Depression. Therefore, if a free economy appears not to be stable, the State has to intervene, fixing limits to the human economic action, although leaving independency to the individual, with the freedom to express his or her own creativity and learning opportunities.

A key aspect to understanding the Animal Spirits and their effects on economic fluctuations is the strong dependency from the compelling correlation with the investment.

> the physical conditions of supply in the capital-goods industries, the state of confidence concerning the prospective yield, the psychological attitude to liquidity and the quantity of money (preferably calculated in terms of wage-units) determine, between them, the rate of new investment. (Keynes, 2006, p. 438)

Such a liaison between economic fluctuation and investment dynamics has to be attributed to the limited knowledge at the base of conventional evaluations of action (Keynes, 2006, p. 322).

'the extreme precariousness of the basis of knowledge on which our estimates of prospective yield have to be made' (Keynes, 2006, p. 309) requires intuition and 'leaps of faith'. This uncertainty creates, in essence, a volatility related to the state of expectations of future investments' yields: since the incentive to invest exists when the expected investment yield is higher than the cost of borrowed money, that is, when the marginal efficiency of the capital is positive, it is evident how the Animal Spirits drive investments by influencing the state of expectations of yields.

We will tackle this issue in Chapter 3, however, it is worth anticipating how the process of acceleration of information circulation is intimately related to the Animal Spirits and potentiates their effects. We are referring to the stock exchange, that, on the one hand, reduces the risks of investments by transforming them into 'liquid' (according to the high possibility of selling and buying stocks compared with the risk of a price variation in a purchase of a batch of physical goods); on the other, it makes investments in their entirety even more uncertain as today investors may buy and lend at a very high speed, in real time, given the digitalization of finance.

DOI: 10.1057/9781137467232.0005

In this perspective of uncertainty and unpredictability, stocks' prices are related to prevalent feelings, which may strikingly fluctuate according to the daily news.

Moreover, the Animal Spirits also affect the level of employment, since, Keynes explains that: 'For unless there is this amount of investment, the receipts of the entrepreneurs will be less than is required to induce them to offer the given amount of employment. It follows, therefore, that, given what we shall call the community's propensity to consume, the equilibrium level of employment, i.e. the level at which there is no inducement to employers as a whole either to expand or to contract employment, will depend on the amount of current investment. The amount of current investment will depend, in turn, on what we shall call the inducement to invest; and the inducement to invest will be found to depend on the relation between the schedule of the marginal efficiency of capital and the complex of rates of interest on loans of various maturities and risks' (Keynes, 2006 p. 212). Such influence finds its explanation in the fact that the decision to invest has a prevailing irrational component.

By observing the current socio-political scenario, just passed into history as the 2008 *subprime mortgages crisis*, it appears that the Animal Spirits, as a specific expression of irrational action, play a determining role in the explanation of its dynamics. The current context of recession, in fact, appears to have broken up the basic assumption of monetarist economics, where contracts are negotiated among rational profit-driven individuals.

According to Akerlof and Shiller (2009) there are five components of the Keynesian Animal Spirits: *confidence*; *fairness* (on which prices and wages depend); *corruption and antisocial behaviour*; *money illusion*; *stories*.

During our reflection, we will tackle each topic separately. We start below to tackle the first issue: confidence.

The elements of trust

Trust and confidence are two concepts widely discussed by scientists and scholars from many different disciplines, including sociology, psychology, behavioural sciences and economics.

They all are aware that these are quite complex constructs. There are two main explanations. First, we may trust for various reasons and with different intensity. For instance, we may trust a person because of his

DOI: 10.1057/9781137467232.0005

or her belonging to a group, or based on our past experience with this person; moreover, we might trust unconditionally or conditionally, in relation to some facts; second, trust is embedded in a system of relationships determining the viral process of cause and effect. For example, the drop in confidence in the ability of some countries to cope with public debt during the 2008 crisis (as Greece, Spain, Italy), reflected in a general loss of confidence towards Europe, the euro and the global financial system – a variation of the levels of trust in specific areas has affected all other parts of the system.

For all these different reasons, we might say that it is not possible to measure trust directly. However, some effects, by materializing their consequences, may be measured.

> It is the return of confidence,..., which is so insusceptible to control in an economy of individualistic capitalism. This is the aspect of the slump which bankers and business men have been right in emphasising, and which the economists who have put their faith in a 'purely monetary' remedy have underestimated. (Keynes, 2006, p. 509)

Although Keynes is able to grasp with sharpness the essence of trust defying any framing, there are three features constantly present in the concept:

1 **Expectations**: Trust has an intrinsic element, that is, projection into the future; conversely, we may say that the future is within trust.

Along with his studies on social exchange, Georg Simmel has been the first scholar to identify the issue of the time–knowledge relationship and relating it to the money exchange perspective. In social interaction, as in the money dynamic, the answer to a proposal arrives in a later moment. Indeed,

> the common relationship that the owner of money and the seller have to a social group – the claim of the former to a service and the trust of the latter that this claim will be honoured – provides the sociological constellation in which money transactions, as distinct from barter, are accomplished. (Simmel, 1987, p. 263)

The supplementary function of trust, therefore, allows money to play its part and enables its circulation. The entire monetary economy rests on such a function of trust, as no one may use money without a line of credit between the two parties. Conferring trust has the meaning of opening a line of credit, where collection is not immediate or explicitly certain (Cotesta, 1998; Pendenza, 2000). Credit, therefore, calls for trust. However, any form of trust implies a leap, an overcoming of distance: thus, time and space dimensions become two essential features of the framing of trust.

As we have outlined in Chapter 1, Simmel explains this latter feature, illustrating the various economic stages of exchange in a teleological series of acts, named the 'economic series of ends'. The sociologist sets a milestone in the issue of trust arguing that

> mere payment in ready cash suggests [...] [that] the stages of the economic series are anxiously compressed, whereas credit creates a distance between them that [he] controls on the basis of trust. (Simmel, 1987, p. 675)

2 **Positive outcome**: The trustor expects that the trustee will allow him or her to reach his or her objectives (Lacohee et al., 2008, p. 17) and will act in a transparent way, refraining from fraud and deception (Simmel, 1987, pp. 295–6).

The expectation of a positive result appears to be a very powerful mechanism in the social and economic environment, as, anticipating an ending which has not yet taken place in reality, allows to act in advance, thus realizing a process of synthesis that accelerates the dynamics in which events occur. For instance, trusting a person, as happens in love or friendship at 'first glance', means expecting a positive feedback today, whereas outcomes will only be confirmed tomorrow – the result is an acceleration in the interaction between the two subjects; in economics, being confident on a positive return on an investment means to increase investments today instead of tomorrow, when we would possibly have more information. The result is the immediate start of a process of acceleration.

3 **Trustworthiness**: or, the free intention to keep relying on the trustee in the future. It appears evident that this feature of trust represents a 'store of value' in the economic sense – in other words, it is a blank cheque for any form of future interaction. Trusted subjects, in fact, are trusted for any commitment or activity. Conversely, distrust is unleashed if the ring of interactions breaks up and the mechanism of reciprocity is compromised, or if the trustee doesn't positively cope with the expectations of the trustor.

DOI: 10.1057/9781137467232.0005

In the 'short-term' speculative mechanism, trust cannot generate value as the intrinsic value of the projection of trust in the future drops. We will see in Chapter 3 how this feature destroys the 'store of value' effect, an element based on which the economic exchange produces efficiencies in the generation of value and accelerates positive influences on processes of real growth.

Besides these three elements characterizing the construct of trust, and in consideration of the systemic condition of the financial market in which we are framing the concept of trust, it is useful for our purposes to make a distinction between institutional trust, systemic trust and interpersonal trust.

▸ **Institutional trust** corresponds to trust in the social system. The latter, intended as a general environment, with society, organizations and people operating in it, represents an expectation of conformity to rules, of stability according to a natural order (Mutti, 1998, p. 38; Durkheim, 1999; Garfinkel, 1983; Parsons, 1965; Luhmann, 1979). Institutional trust is granted by acknowledging a major role within the social system to the institution against the single individual. This is justified by the control of a greater wealth of information, supported by higher competencies. Keynes maintains, in that respect, that the role of institutions, such as the Treasury and the Bank of England, lies in freeing people from the mistrust based on the assignment of value to money by a voluntary decision.

▸ **Systemic trust** is a concept quite close to the previous one, however it emphasizes the conditions of those highly complex contexts such as the global economy. By operating a 'reduction of the complexity of the system' (Luhmann, 1979), the systemic trust operates an identification of focused expectations and motivations – trust on a rating agency such as Standard & Poor's or Fitch, is a case in point. These rating agencies simplify and filter information by operating a 'reduction of social complexity' (Luhmann, 2001). It is worth mentioning that, because of their position, they also enjoy institutional trust.

▸ **Interpersonal trust** is tied to social and professional roles and persons. It is the trust we may find in the relationship between a dealer in financial assets and their customer. Within the communication process between the two actors, uncertainty may

DOI: 10.1057/9781137467232.0005

stem from the interpretation and expectations of one, built on the expectations of the other. This process may be called a 'double contingency' of social interaction. In this case, trust recurs as an expectation of regularity and continuity in the behavioural role and in the actors' identity (Mutti, 1998, pp. 40–1).

Indeed, more often, the three forms of trust melt together – a way to simplify complexity is operated through the space–time reduction of action by limiting it to communities or defined places: virtual financial communities or financial marketplaces such as the City of London, or Wall Street in New York are 'interpretative communities' (Mutti, 1998, p. 58), providing cognitive and emotional support to trust initiatives and decisions made by a simultaneous physical presence and the direct interaction of many actors. The exclusive networks of the financial élites are restricted circles of interaction where trust, confirmed over time by membership and a sense of belonging, and direct or virtual participation, accelerates the decision-making processes. Here, again, interpersonal trust is activated thanks to simultaneous physical presence and the direct interaction of many actors. Hence, a real interaction integrates with the virtual one, thus connecting the two systems.

Besides these three typologies of trust, there are five other dimensions that are intrinsic to the construct of trust, which contribute to a clearer definition of the concept (McKnight, et al., 1996), these are: *Competence, Benevolence, Integrity, Transparency and Identification or Value Congruence.* These elements are not separable as they must be present and complete, all at the same time. In other words, a government, an institution, or a person cannot gain trustworthiness from another person or institution showing just competence whilst lacking integrity or transparency.

Let's analyse these items:

Competence: When we talk about competence, we refer to two sides of the same coin: on the one side, the technical competence that through specific abilities allows the effective achievement of objectives; on the other, the organizational and managerial side, including also the aspects regarding the management of resources, both tangible and human. Competence is evaluated through performance or results, which if positive, definitely helps the trust-building process. The Edelman Trust Barometer (see Chapter 1) indicates that 86% of respondents state that if companies ensure quality control in their products, this fact will have its greatest impact in the engagement, integrity and perception of both the quality and innovation of the companies' products.[10]

Benevolence: benevolence is the will of the trustee to care about the trustor, far from profit and personal interest motivations (Mayer et al., 1995, p. 176).

This concept is tied to the topic of 'doing good', to altruism, to a positive relationship between trustor and trustee and a genuine will to be open/to be ready to acknowledge any need of the other party, generating an authentic relationship. Benevolence represents the most 'social' intentional side of the construct of trust and, as such, it has a particular relevance. The sociological paradigm of reference is the Simmelian interaction and the 'gift' (Ricœur, 2005; Caillé, 1998; Zamagni, 2007). Interaction explains the sense of reciprocity ingenerated via a benevolent attitude, which entails a process of circulation of goods and actions; the gift, as maintained by Alain Caillé, refers to an act of gratuity as freed from the part of duty. This notion is present, instead, in the concept of Latin *munus*, intended as role, position: the *muni*ficence of 'the more I give, the more I am' – it is nothing but an expression of power. For instance, let's take the relationship of a municipality and its citizens. If a citizen realizes that public initiatives with social aims are introduced as a result of a municipality's autonomous decision, as aid to the poor or specific environmental services, these initiatives will result in a stimulus to reciprocity, reinforcing civic minded attitudes, a sense of belonging, and, finally, trust towards the institution.

Integrity: if benevolence is a feeling that cannot be framed as an ethical norm, integrity represents the moral side of a behaviour. Integrity implies '[...] the trustor's perception that the trustee adheres to a set of principles that the trustor finds acceptable' (Mayer et al., 1995, p. 719). This feature of trust requires a strong coherence with past actions, a solid reputation that is credible, linked to positive actions by others, and a sense of justice and coherence between words and facts: then trust may build. We have introduced the topic of reputation in the previous chapter; in this chapter and the next we will tackle the reasons why deceit and corruption breed in strongly deregulated contexts and in parallel financial markets, where the face of the finance actors is easily deceivable. In such a climate the value of honesty and transparency (this we will tackle as the next point) becomes a key element in the reputation of organizations: the 2014 Edelman Trust

DOI: 10.1057/9781137467232.0005

Barometer indicates that integrity is the second key attribute, after engagement, to build trust.

Transparency: Transparency represents the possibility of the trustor to obtain information about the trustee's integrity. No doubt it's a hot topic as it concerns the will of organizations and institutions to be 'controlled' by the public. This process, by design, allows a more definite and empathically perceptible identity, to the advantage of the person (trustor)–institution (trustee) relationship. Information, moreover, allows a rational evaluation of the trustworthiness, by supporting a positive image of the trustee.

The lack of transparency is interpreted as being the intention to hide some facts or behaviours that could damage the integrity of a trustee's position. Corruption, for instance, automatically pushes towards closure or distortion of information and when it emerges, it corrupts trust.

Identification or Value Congruence: the process of identification, as Ricœur argues, is the first of three phases leading to reciprocity.[11] Identification also implies integration and sharing: a key premise to establish that involvement or engagement, allowing the building of value over time through a relationship of reciprocity. As a matter of fact, Simmel explains that identity is intrinsically tied to the concept of difference: ego cannot exist if its boundaries aren't drawn by the *alter*.[12] It's just this ego–alter interaction that creates the community.

We have already drawn some features of the complex construct of trust. First, the three basic elements of the concept, which are: expectation, positive result, reliability; then, we have made a distinction between various typologies of trust, differentiating them into: institutional, systemic and interpersonal; finally, we have pointed out the attributes of the construct or 'trust beliefs': Competence, Benevolence, Integrity, Transparency, Identification or Value Congruence.

Now we can move to the key distinction between the concept of *trust* and *confidence*. This partition (Padua, 2012) allows the planting of the concept of trust in a ground most suited to our discussion: we refer to the conditions of uncertainty or certainty.

The first typology of trust involves irrational and emotional elements, establishing a reciprocal interaction among the actors without any rational basis. It operates in conditions of uncertainty on the outcome of the trust relationship and of the lack of control over the outcomes of the action.

DOI: 10.1057/9781137467232.0005

The second typology, on the other hand, refers to a concept tied to rational, quantitative evaluations, complying with a one-way process, different from the two-directional process occurring in the course of interaction. As an example, it is useless to talk about reciprocity with regard to having confidence that the prices of some securities will rise, based on forecasts calculated on the past course. Rationality, grounded on information, which represents the bricks of logical reasoning, offers guarantees on the control of the outcomes. This is an objective result, as it complies with a calculation.

In its purest form, confidence matches the principles of the Rational Choice Theory, grounded on perfect information. However, it is relevant to highlight that between trusting and being confident there is a form of in-between trust, which puts together rational and irrational factors. This distinction produces three levels of trust: the first is totally irrational; the second is totally rational (confidence); the third is an intermediate form of trust that we name 'rational trust' (Padua, 2012). We are now going to tackle these three levels.

Trust, confidence, and rational trust

To provide a definition to both the dimensions of trust and confidence let us recall the three cornerstones discussed above: expectation, positive result and reliability.

Trust

In trusting, the expectation lies within the answer to an offer of trust that took place in a previous moment. We are anyway in a state of risk, generated by the lack of information apt to eliminate the hazard: in a condition of total lack of information, trust takes shape as 'blind relying' or a 'leap of faith', as Simmel clarifies (Simmel, 1987). For example, we trust in God or in a Nation.

The second cornerstone of trust, the expectation of a positive result, shows itself to be full, as trusting bears a state of positivity, indeed, not excluding the states of uncertainty in which the expectation grows up: the one who trusts accepts that there is a risk, that is, there are chances that the trustee may betray his or her trust, as there is no guarantee on the outcomes. Moreover, such a condition of uncertainty, is furthermore

DOI: 10.1057/9781137467232.0005

reinforced by the inability on the part of the trustor to control the trustee: he or she is totally disempowered.

A remarkable feature of trusting lies in the sense of 'reciprocity' established between the parties. There can be no trust between two actors
if there is no recognition of the priority of the other party. In other
words, during the first steps of a trust relationship, the trustor makes, in
advance, his or her judgement on the trustee, who enjoys a position of
priority (Padua, 2012).

In such a framework, the normative side of trust emerges, grounded
on the social paradigm expressed by Simmel as the 'faith of a man in
another man' (Poggi, 1998, p. 299). This feature, giving trust a role of
norm and a guarantee of interaction, appears particularly relevant in the
analysis of the current economic context.

The situation of crisis, in fact, and the preponderance of Nominal
Economy, generates a gap of distrust with institutions whereas the
normative component should appear solid. In the speculative market,
instead, trust works as a guarantee within interaction, generating closer
relationships among dealers and their customers, such as individuals
or hedge funds, in bilateral trading. In this way, as the one-to-one trust
relationship prevails over the trust in institutions (institutional trust), if
we apply this concept to the metaphor of the chain (see p. 32), any ring of
the chain becomes separate towards the other parts of the chain, resulting in a lack of responsibility (see Chapter 1, Nominal Economy vs. Real
Economy, 'Lack of responsibility', p. 32). Here we remind that the highest
distance is between the issuer and the owner of the title.

Thanks to these features, trust is at the base of social interaction
(Simmel, 1987), building, over time, a circular process of reciprocity,
influence and exchange (Giddens, 1994).

The third cornerstone of trust, reliability, projects a renewed chance of
trusting in the future.

Confidence

In contrast with the concept of trust, in its highly irrational meaning,
the pure idea of confidence corresponds to an expectation of a positive
outcome in conditions of certainty, influenced by basic indicators and
probabilities built on past experiences. Such a certainty derives from
an availability of information sufficient to grant the positive outcome
of the expectation and from the position of power versus the trustee.

DOI: 10.1057/9781137467232.0005

This takes place to the extent of excluding the risk tied to Simmelian irrationality. The objectivity of certainty provides interesting food for thought. It comes from controllable quantitative data, conforming to reality and to objective knowledge, shared by all. Undoubtedly, the confidence of the analysts of the Chicago school[13] was a form of perfect confidence in the correctness of the econometric models. Such an 'objective' certainty, irrefutable, broke down in September 2008: it wasn't just a financial slump, it was *a breakdown in the confidence in the certainties of objectivity*: suddenly, reality appeared just as a mental construction.

Many understood that it was *a* reality, not *the* reality.

This assumption allows us to introduce the third typology of trust, named 'Rational trust' to highlight the coexistence of irrational and rational factors.

Rational trust

As we have said, between pure trust and pure confidence, between instinct and logic, there is an intermediate form of trust.[14]

This is a hybrid form of confidence that we define as 'rational trust': it reflects most situations in which it is evident that owned information doesn't offer guarantees of a positive outcome. However, it works on a decisional basis that try to at least reduce risks. As an example, it may occur in those cases where we rely on a financial dealer to make an investment: we have information on the level of trustworthiness of the society and on the reliability of the dealer from our social network and from quantitative data, but we don't have any failsafe method of knowing whether there is a risk that he or she might abscond with our money, or about his or her competencies in finding the most profitable investment.

Reality, indeed, shows us that a leap of faith has certainly been made. However, it has been done on the basis of limited information and no form of control may be exerted: therefore, it is commonly shared that there is a sort of vulnerability (Hart, 1989). In these cases it may be said that the trustor has used a level of 'reasonable', cautious and wise knowledge (Latouche, 2000; Mauss, 2002; Sen, 2001).

As in the case of confidence, rational trust becomes a form of trust that operates a meaningful bond between the past and the future, where information used came from *past experience* whilst expectations stand for *future projection*.

DOI: 10.1057/9781137467232.0005

As past experience, we might also mean a proven reliability, tested over time. Moreover, it may happen that rational trust starts with a leap of faith, confirmed over time by positive experiences. In this situation, past experience works on an informative basis from which logical reasoning on probabilities and possibilities of control may be exerted: here we are moving towards a 'pure' form of confidence.

On the future projection standpoint, it is worth highlighting how the 'management of expectations' is a key tool of the political economy in building or re-building trust. It is not just a datum to be analysed and transformed into an index.

Positive expectation is an intrinsic part of trust and it lies at the heart of the two-way relationship established between two subjects. Without the belief to accomplish our expectations there can't be any form of reciprocity. Even if we talk about expectations of people towards government, it is worthwhile highlighting the existence of a feature of dependency of the trustee on the trustor within a trust relationship: it represents the obligation to return the trust given, that is, the obligation to reciprocity. The trustor has the power to control the course of action of the trustee, and based on that fact, he or she evaluates whether the promises are kept: the voter has power over the elected and is in the position to confirm his or her consensus.

To substantiate this form of intermediate 'trust', the wide literature available (Mutti, 1998; Cotesta, 1998; Pendenza, 2000) explains that trust generates, at large, in a situation of uncertainty about reality and its future outcomes. In his masterpiece, *Soziologie*, Simmel specifies that on this ground of absence of certainties, trust works in an intermediate area between 'complete ignorance' and 'complete knowledge' (Simmel, 1987, p. 299). In other words, we don't use trust, and neither do we when we have complete information, because there would be no need for faith, nor when we are in complete ignorance, as it would be too hazardous. Under the cognitive perspective, therefore, trust represents a solution to the absence of information and to the lack of control on reality, usually carried out by knowledge. In this perspective, in which trust balances this lack of information, it gains a character of rationality, by transforming into a calculation of probabilities, that is, into a bet. It is easy to understand how this concept is tightly connected to the notion of risk, as it relates probabilities of success to the costs of possible losses.

We ask ourselves, therefore, what is Keynes' position on the issue of trust?

DOI: 10.1057/9781137467232.0005

Keynes does not only have doubts about the existence of certainties within reality, as it results from actions driven by irrational instincts, but the economist furthermore challenges the ability of 'reading' reality: we have seen, in fact, how economic actors act in conditions of highly uncertain information.

This basic assumption has influenced the Keynesian theory of long-term expectations, a key factor in investment decisions. To Keynes,

> Business men play a mixed game of skill and chance, the average results of which to the players are not known by those who take a hand. If human nature felt no temptation to take a chance, no satisfaction (profit apart) in constructing a factory, a railway, a mine or a farm, there might not be much investment merely as a result of cold calculation. (Keynes, 2006, p. 336)

In other words it appears that economic development is in the hands of the Animal Spirits of businessmen.

Based on this consideration we may say that the concept of trust in Keynes plays a major role: it arises within the concept of Animal Spirits and takes shape in price determination in relation to the state of long-term expectations, influencing, in turn, the level of income and unemployment.[15]

Once more, the key role of trust in the government (or non-government ...) of the economy comes to light.

The role of emotions

Based on what has been said, has trust to be considered a calculation or a feeling?

Within these two alternatives lies the strong contrast between trust intended as relying or as a leap of faith and confidence.

We have already considered how Keynes puts irrational behaviour in a leading position.

The emotional and irrational approach of the Animal Spirits in the economic action hasn't come to a halt with Keynes. It represents a new interpretation that behavioural economics has embraced, giving rise to a new line of thought that progressively is taking hold in the scientific community.

Let us see which are the values behind this decision-making process along this perspective.

DOI: 10.1057/9781137467232.0005

The 'psychology of decision' leads the behavioural economists to isolate the causes of the main economic decisions in the processes of 'mental' nature. This viewpoint opposes, for obvious reasons, all those mathematic interpretations, complex and distant from the human emotions of many economists, and based on 'technical factors and governmental decisions' (Motterlini and Guala, 2005, p. 5).

The School of Behavioural Economics and Experimental Economics is grounded on the basic assumption enlightened by the behavioural studies on the existence of a gap between 'human behaviour and theories, decision psychology and logic of decision' (Egidi, 2005, p. XI).

To understand the gap between the Schools of Behavioural and Experimental economics and Rational Choice Theory we should consider that the rational choice theory, on which the theory of value which prevailed in the twentieth century is based, maintains that the individual takes actions that lead to specific consequences. The theory upholds that the individual is in the position to figure out all possible consequences and to be able to make an 'order of preferences' among them by a rational calculation. At that time, however, early empirical experiments on decision-making processes began to make their way, showing results contrasting to the rational choice theory's assumptions. The Chicago school of Milton Friedman tried to absorb and mediate, though in a limited way and with difficulties, the diversity of decision-making processes through procedures aggregating large-scale processes. However, the rational choice theory was put into discussion more vigorously by Herbert Simon's theory of 'limited rationality', during the first part of the 1950s: the Weberian models of bureaucracy rooted on the rational action, marked time in the highly uncertain contexts where businessmen were operating during that period.

It was already highly improbable in those circumstances to own the knowledge of all possible decisions. Simon, with his theory rejecting the possibility of reaching a perfect information, has undoubtedly the merit to have brought to light the relevance of the reconstruction of the decision-making context through which information is taken, and allowing the building of knowledge.

The mental representation is moulded on this process of design of the decisional context (Egidi, 2005, p. XV) that is evidently empirical as well as intuitive; moreover, the context is not even comprehensible as it is constantly dynamic.

DOI: 10.1057/9781137467232.0005

The relevance of the role of the context has already been highlighted when we discussed Keynes as the economist of complexity. We have seen how Keynes' view of the economic context is organic and complex. This approach represents a clear overcoming of the linear cause-effect explanation of reality of the Rational Choice Theory. In Chapter 3 we will tackle again the role of the context when we will discuss the matter of probability and the Keynesian convention.

This means that subjects act in relation to their cognitive perception which may be different from reality. This means that people trust what they perceive and their beliefs. The cognitive perspective, in fact, is different from the objective viewpoint as it is based on subjective perception and interpretation. Indeed, being the perception subjective, it may be quite different from real facts. In the decision-making processes, in the various stages of representation, in the process of editing[16] and the construction of mental models, what influences the decision is the context in which the decision is made (Egidi, 2005, p. XVII). Experiments have shown how a same subject shows a different attitude to risk in relation to the context in which the decision is made.

Cognitivists explain, indeed, why the context plays an essential role to the building of trust.

Trust in social systems

After having outlined the features and the composition of the trust construct, in this paragraph, we start to coordinate the concept with the socio-economic reality on which our reflection is grounded. These reflections prepare the ground for Chapter 3 in which we will shed light on the issue of the Economy of Trust.

The philosopher and sociologist, Georg Simmel, argues that 'exchange is one of the functions that creates an inner bond between men – a society, in place of a mere collection of individuals' (Simmel, 1987, p. 258).

Trust is the basis of this dynamic of exchange and regulates social order (Barber, 1983) through the creation of social cohesion, the binding agent of society.[17]

The first conclusion we may draw to the aim of a 'social' interpretation of the role of trust within the current economic system is the existence of (a) a tight connection between cognitive and emotional features of trust in the various forms of money and (b) the role of the social network inside which the intersection of financial demand and supply is determined. The growing and pervasive presence of technology makes the analysis of socio-economic networks even more complex. This is why we talk of techno-social networks (Berra, 2007), whereas technology adds complexity in terms of further acceleration of the processes.

Understanding the techno-social network on which the economic exchanges take place, nowadays at a global level, it is essential to understand how the global economy works as it is key to defining the space–time dimension. Individuating and understanding how financial networks operate means, in fact, to identify the social and cultural determinants that provide an interpretation of two aspects: on the one side, information related to 'inductive knowledge' (the Simmelian knowledge logic) on which the economic decision forecasts are grounded; on the other, emotional and psychological aspects influencing behaviours. It deals with discourses, stories and symbols generated inside the networks, with relations of power to influence the course of expectations and of 'expectations of expectations'. Consequently, the symbols of the 2008 crisis represent extremely interesting elements of analysis.

We may also find them in the 'epic' movie production of greedy financial businessmen, businessmen as the protagonists of 'Wall Street'; others may be found in the global financial marketplaces where their decisions influence leading stock exchange indexes; many others may be found in other places where 'the fallen debt is transformed into a permanent profitable activity' and where, as Bauman maintains (Bauman, 2011, p. 9), banks foster debt with other debt.

The issue related to the social aspects of the financial networks and to the risk of disintegration of the latter into a state of crisis lies in the fact that 'the expansion and the duration of a financial network represents an index of trustworthiness itself' (Mutti, 1998, p. 56). This became evident during the 2008 crisis when everyone trusted a system that, notwithstanding any skilled expectation, in the end showed itself to be deeply unreliable.

One of the reasons for this illusion lies in the intrinsic structural weakness of the system: the system is not a single entity. It is, instead, kept together only by the links of an enormous number of 'chains of acts of interpersonal trust'. As we have already discussed, the single ring (the relationship between a dealer and a customer) is not able to check the starting point and the end of the 'chain' that we have described as a series of financial buy-and-sell exchanges (Chapter 1). For this reason, the

DOI: 10.1057/9781137467232.0005

relationship remains isolated in an interpersonal (or person-to-business or business-to-business) exchange which lacks general vision, key to evaluating the level of hazard.

In other words, as in the Simmelian 'teleological series' of acts, the complexity of the financial products, the continuous re-designing of the offers, and their constant aggregation and reconfiguration in relation to the demand of the financial market make their breakdown into single elementary components extremely difficult. For this reason it is impossible to track back the sources of these elements in a reliable way: the knowledge gap between the issuer and the owner of the security becomes so wide as determined by a sequence of exchanges that it doesn't allow for obtaining a set of information able to reduce the hazard.

This phenomenon has been further reinforced by the proliferation of complex financial products such as the securitization of the subprime securities in a system in which securities substitute money, therefore becoming a symbol of a virtual liquidity.

This process comes from the progressive replacement of the traditional role of money in favour of financial products acting just like currency, with the consequence, as we have seen in the previous chapter, of misplacing social relationships.

To summarize, the *trust in money*, discussed above, is tied to three entities: first, to the trust in 'government' that guarantees the value of exchange; second, to 'institutions' responsible for regulating the stability of such value; third, to the 'community'. Conversely, *trust in securities* refers to the generalized trust towards the 'networks' in which they circulate and to 'interpersonal' trust: we trust the person selling us the financial product or we trust the system from where we directly purchase that product (i.e., a stock exchange digital marketplace) and the information and perception that we may get from either the person or the organization selling the product.

In other words, if trust in the value of €1000 in currency is founded on the reliability of the government, on the buying power of that amount of money (here we cannot help but remember the power of money illusion), and on the relationship between the two individuals exchanging currency, the ownership of €1000 in investment funds makes its value trustworthy in relation to a different item: that is, to the financial system tied to the level of reliability of the network of the investment companies linked to the owned securities (i.e., owners of other investment funds influencing the level of the price of the funds owned by the person).

DOI: 10.1057/9781137467232.0005

Such trustworthiness depends on the rational and irrational evaluation of the network, which lies in the hands of the symbolic elements and of the interpretive processes shared through that specific techno-social network within the marketplace.

In a vacuum of institutional power as the one generated within the global financial network before and during the 2008 crisis of the 2008 crisis, the control has been taken either by restricted circles of élites or it was fragmented into a number of one-to-one relationships such as the ones regulated by interpersonal trust built between the dealers and customers of subprime bonds. With these isolated relationships bonded to a quite limited scope of individual information (for example, the individuals purchasing mortgage securities to invest their little savings from a financial broker), two separate outcomes are generated: the first is that the 'weak ring' has become subject to the robust influence of irrational actions of the collective behaviours – this situation of weakness has played a key role in the upsurge of the speculative bubble generated by a general impetus of panic and then in the following burst; the second consequence is the actors' general lack of responsibility within the process at any level, as we have discussed in previous chapter.

On a purely ethical note, we ought to ask ourselves why those who knew about the hazards that accompany a speculative bubble, did not act.

Beyond any easy considerations of greed and 'profit at any cost', of phenomena of organized deception by some financial institutions which have been prosecuted by law after the crash of 2008, the lack of status and power of institutions to invert the perverse dynamic of the whole 'financial chain' has to be highlighted. This would have led to the breaking up of a process supported and validated by the totality of the networks and kept together by influent dense reticles of powerful financial businessmen belonging to restricted financial circuits. These subjects, in the absence of a regulation (norms and sanctions), create their own norms.

In essence, the agreements among these individuals make 'losing the adherence to principles' (Becker, 1983) appear rational and justified. We may, therefore, argue that trust in highly complex contexts shows an *ambivalent* attitude: on the one side, it tends to de-personalize (lose the relationship with the individual actor) and decontextualize (lose contact with the general environment), finding the dimension of a 'form of generalized trust' as the only way out. It deals with an institutional or systemic trust, delegated to agents skilled in 'filtering and simplification'

DOI: 10.1057/9781137467232.0005

(i.e., rating agencies); at the same time, with the aim of self-generating, it tends to localize itself (as in financial real and virtual marketplaces), to personalize (by the relationship between dealer and customer), and to find cognitive and emotional elements appropriate to develop its rational and irrational bases.

There's also another reflection: having trust a systemic character, that is, being viral and contagious, a leak or sudden loss of trust in a remote part of the system may determine a drop in generalized trust that will influence the interpersonal trust relationships between credit owners and debt owners. Media and expert systems in this case, as in many others, work as a sounding board as well as propagate the information based upon which the rational side of trust is built, playing a strategic role in the generation of trust itself.

In this perspective, interpersonal and generalized trust appears to be interlinked where the first appears to be the basis for the second one in highly complex systems; and the second influences the first in a general way.

These last reflections allow us to complete the picture of the networks of actors that, according to a definition by Thrift (Thrift, 1996) characterize the socio-techno-cultural system on which trust in the financial-economic system is rooted: *governments*; *media* as online or offline press, radio, television; rating agencies; financial capitalists; and expert systems belonging to the network.

However, something has changed since the work of Thrift was published.

Rating agencies can't be included among media, as they are nowadays playing the full role of financial actors. It is not an informative intermediary position anymore: they are agents of primary relevance for trust and speculative policies. This role is run via the definition and diffusion of rankings on the levels of reliability (and, reversely, of risk levels) of financial products and nations' sovereignty. The latter evaluation is made in relation to the ability of States to cover their public debt and deficit (Wilson A. et al., 2012) limiting possible downsizing risks for international investors. The seriousness of the consequences of these actions are very severe, as a bad rating may lead to a threat to the legitimacy of the institutional order and to a decline of the social capital of a nation. Such a threat is explained by the positive bond between institutional trust (relying on institutions because of their higher position and competence versus the single individual) and interpersonal trust.

DOI: 10.1057/9781137467232.0005

Researchers have indicated that a drop in the level of systemic and institutional trust (Lipset and Schneider, 1983) brings a drop in self-confidence and in confidence with other persons. In turn, such a drop influences negatively the institutional legitimacy.

The proposal of the UK Prime Minister, David Cameron, to revitalize the middle social organizations as the networks of civic associations, and the spontaneous communities of mutual aid via a Big Society, was an attempt to rebuild the precious social capital legacy via a strong investment in interpersonal trust. Nevertheless, the aims of the Big Society have been queried and disputed and the concept has received criticism from many sides of the political spectrum.

With this topic about the shift between interpersonal and institutional trust we are going to open the next subject, the Economy of Trust.

Notes

1   J.M. Keynes (2006[1936]).
2   Monetarism is a school of economic thought that maintains that the money supply (the total amount of money in an economy, in the form of coin, currency, and bank deposits) is the chief determinant on the demand side of short-run economic activity. American economist Milton Friedman is generally regarded as monetarism's leading exponent. Friedman and other monetarists advocate a macroeconomic theory and policy that diverge significantly from those of the formerly dominant Keynesian school. The monetarist approach became influential during the 1970s and early 1980s (http://www.britannica.com, accessed 8 June 2014).
3   The 'prisoners' dilemma' is the best-known game of strategy in social science, originated within the Game Theory. It helps us to understand what governs the balance between cooperation and competition in business, in politics, and in social settings.
      In the traditional version of the game, the police have arrested two suspects and are interrogating them in separate rooms. Each can either confess, thereby implicating the other, or keep silent. No matter what the other suspect does, each can improve his own position by confessing. If the other confesses, then one had better do the same to avoid the especially harsh sentence that awaits a recalcitrant holdout. If the other keeps silent, then one can obtain the favourable treatment accorded a state's witness by confessing. Thus, confession is the dominant strategy for each. But when both confess, the outcome is worse for both than when both keep silent. The concept of the prisoners' dilemma was developed by RAND Corporation

scientists Merrill Flood and Melvin Dresher and was formalized by Albert W. Tucker, a Princeton mathematician (http://www.econlib.org, accessed 8 June 2014).

4   Pareto explained the individual action by two forms of action: logical and non-logical. The first category consists of rational actions whose end is objective, supported by rational calculation. Non-logical actions, instead, have a non-rational end due to their subjective nature, that is, tied to what the subject believes in, feels, and thinks is right. Pareto assumes that social action is mainly driven by this latter category of actions (Padua, 2010, p. 29).

5   The Animal Spirits are similar to the Simmelian paradigm of religious faith. They are impulses with no rational basis.

6   These theoretical contributions represent the ground where the network analysis, a branch of the Methodology of Social Sciences, developed.

7   Gustave Le Bon is one of the first sociologists to study crowd behaviour. In our reflection, the coherence with the Keynesian systemic approach led to the application of the same paradigm to the financial realm.

8   Pareto equates the social system to a net of elastic intertwined strings put together by plumb bobs. Moving even just one, the whole system modifies its setting. The essence of the social system, therefore, is the relationship between the elements and their levels of balance (Padua, 2010, p. 2).

9   Deficit spending together with the Multiplier of investment form the most distinctive tool of political economics bequeathed by the General Theory (Skidelski, 1996).

10   http://www.edelman.com, accessed 6 June 2014.

11   Ricœur explains the sense of reciprocity in the dimension of the gift according to three stages: identification, validation, gratitude. Identity, implicating a process of identification, is the first step of every process of reciprocity.

12   The concept of identity via subtraction develops alongside the Hegelian doctrine, through Marx.

13   The Chicago school of economics is a neoclassical school of economic thought associated with the work of the faculty at the University of Chicago, some of whom have constructed and popularized its principles. In the context of macroeconomics, it is connected to the freshwater school of macroeconomics, in contrast to the saltwater school based in coastal universities (notably Harvard, MIT and Berkeley). Chicago macroeconomic theory rejected Keynesianism in favour of monetarism right up until the mid-1970s, when it turned to new classical macroeconomics heavily based on the concept of rational expectations (http://en.wikipedia.org, accessed 15 June 2014).

14   Simmel, in his Philosophy of Money, highlights an ambivalent character in the concept of trust, both cognitive and normative. By analysing trust

DOI: 10.1057/9781137467232.0005

in the form of credit, the sociologist maintains that it shows different viewpoints: on the one side, it is composed of an 'inductive' knowledge, comparable to the one of the merchant, who won't buy goods if he or she thought it would not sell; or the farmer if he or she wouldn't sow the field if it wasn't expected to produce a good crop. On the other hand, another kind of trust exists which, in its purest form, finds expression as 'religious faith', a 'further element of socio-psychological nature' (Simmel, 1984, p. 264) similar to a faith in God. This kind of trust not only reflects a limited knowledge, but a different state of mind 'something more and something less' (Simmel, 1984). When we say 'I trust someone', it's similar to beginning a relationship and the difference between our perception of this person and the existence of the person. It is a certainty in entrusting ourselves to this entity, stemming from recognizable reasons, but it doesn't consist in them. Also economic credit often contains an element of this metatheoretical faith, the same takes place when we trust that the community will give us tangible value in exchange for symbolic signs through which we have exchanged the fruits of our work, and, likewise, that cash may be used in a later moment.

15 Keynes maintains that 'We have seen above that the marginal efficiency of capital depends, not only on the existing abundance or scarcity of capital-goods and the current cost of production of capital-goods, but also on current expectations as to the future yield of capital-goods. In the case of durable assets it is, therefore, natural and reasonable that expectations of the future should play a dominant part in determining the scale on which new investment is deemed advisable. But, as we have seen, the basis for such expectations is very precarious. Being based on shifting and unreliable evidence, they are subject to sudden and violent changes' (Keynes, 1971–89, p. 116).

16 In behavioural economics, the Prospect theory is a behavioural economic theory that describes the way people choose among probabilistic alternatives that involve risk, where the probabilities of outcomes are known. The theory states that people make decisions based on the potential value of losses and gains rather than the final outcome, and that people evaluate these losses and gains using certain heuristics. The theory describes the decision-making processes in two stages: editing and evaluation. During editing, outcomes of a decision are ordered according to a certain heuristic. In particular, people decide which outcomes they consider equivalent, set a reference point, and then consider lesser outcomes as losses and greater ones as gains. (http://en.wikipedia.org, accessed 9 June 2014).

17 Such a concept recalls the notion of 'organic solidarity' holding society together. In *The Philosophy of Money* (Simmel, 1987), the issue of trust emerges as a constituent element of society (Blau et al., 1967) that has inspired many

sociologists such as Garfinkel, Luhmann and Giddens (Garfinkel, 2004; Luhmann, 1979; Giddens, 1994).

DOI: 10.1057/9781137467232.0005

3
Value

Abstract: *Why does trust collapse during crises? What are the consequences? How is it possible to build value based on trust? Padua attempts to provide answers via the original concept of 'Economy of Trust', or the process of value building though a prevalent trust component in complex socio-economic systems, accelerated by speculative contexts and in conditions of uncertainty. The Economy of Trust, reflecting the economic context within the current 2008 recession through the social behaviour of the individual, contains the essence of Keynesian thought. It builds value by replacing guarantees in deregulated contexts and in situations of loss of institutional power. There are five sociological reasons behind the development of the Economy of Trust in a Nominal economy: uncertainty, irrationality, speculation, complexity and stories.*

Keywords: 2008 crisis and recession; building value through trust; complex socio-economic systems; speculation; stories; uncertainty and irrationality in economics

Padua, Donatella. *John Maynard Keynes and the Economy of Trust: The Relevance of the Keynesian Social Thought in a Global Society.* Basingstoke: Palgrave Macmillan, 2014. DOI: 10.1057/9781137467232.0006.

In 2009, in the United States of America, trust suffered a sudden collapse. Along the wave of the economic downturn, all institutions were involved, making trust indicators dramatically drop against 2008:[1] in business, indicators plummeted from 59% to 36% (−23%); in ONGs, from 63% to 45% (−18%); in government from 43% to 30% (−13%); and in media, from 46% to 31% (−15%). To the question 'how much do you trust institutions to do what is right?' respondents have answered in a sensibly negative way against the previous year. In particular, the survey highlights an occurrence which never emerged during the previous twelve years' surveys: trust in governments has dropped to a historical minimum: 52% of respondents who, in 2010, had stated they 'trust their government', in 2011 dramatically dropped to 43%, indicating a fall of 9%. In Japan, Russia and Spain indicators have plummeted even beyond 30%.

These facts lead us to ask some necessary questions:

> Why does trust fall during crises? What are the consequences? How is it possible to build value on trust? How is it possible to regain trust?

Given the complexity of the question, it appears particularly difficult to provide safe responses; nevertheless, the aim of this chapter is to isolate some key features about the reasons for the drop in trust and the possible fallouts. The topic of the building or the retrieval of trust will be tackled in the next chapter and in the conclusions.

To grasp the correlation between a socio-economic crisis and the drop in trust indicators, we introduce the innovative concept of the 'Economy of Trust'.

The specific aim of the first part of the following reflection is to connect this concept to the mainframe of the Nominal Economy and global economy. In the following paragraphs, however, we will try to deepen the functioning of the Economy of Trust by relating the original notion to some key sociological dimensions of the construct of trust: uncertainty, irrationality, speculation, complexity and stories.

The Economy of Trust in the global crisis

In a 'nominal economy', the power exerted by trust is extremely influential.

According to its etymology, the term 'economy' comes from the term *ôikos*, which means home, asset and extensive house economy, and *nomos*, relating to rule, law: the term refers, therefore, to the art of managing and soundly administering private and public assets.[2] Nevertheless, we have seen how in the current Nominal Economy, assets management has no regulations. This reveals two reasons: according to the first, the main responsibility for the lack of regulation is to be traced to the liberal economic paradigm, whose origin is considered by many economists to be found in the growth of un-regulated markets; the second one refers to the intersecting of two phenomena: the huge volume of money exchanged in un-regulated markets and the complexity of the technological network through which money flows. It appears quite evident that an objective inability to control may occur in such a nominal economic regimen. As an additional result, the frequent absence of rule compliance generates an anomic condition, as the sociologist Émile Durkheim would define it, where often fraud adds up to deceit.

Within this typical Nominal Economy mainframe, the 'Economy of Trust' finds its origin. Our aim, therefore, is to try to understand how the Keynesian theory may contribute to this concept. Keynes, in contrast to the experts of his time, assigns to trust a key role in the economy. The Economist argues that this behavioural variable exerts a highly relevant influence on the level of the marginal efficiency of the capital. In other words, trust lies at the base of the prospective trend of capital, which, as seen, is influenced by expectations. Expectations and trust, therefore, are intrinsically linked not only to the domain of expected profits but also to investments. Indeed, the marginal efficiency of the capital is directly related to the demand of investment. The Keynesian trust builds value, not by accomplishing the rules of the value theory of classical thought but by complying with the Keynesian assumption that integrates the value theory with money, assets and goods markets.

As the aim of this volume is to provide the reader with a sociological interpretation of the current economic picture, the concept of the Economy of Trust is designed to provide an explanation of the economic realm through the elements tightly related to the behaviour of the individual. The content of Chapters 1 and 2 encourages us to concentrate our attention on the aspects of irrationality and Keynesian trust within the relationships between social actors.

To the extent of providing an explanation of what the Economy of Trust is, let us first of all try to define the concept:

> The Economy of trust is the process of value building based on the exchange of goods and services realized though a prevalent trust component: it

substantiates in the set of spontaneous trust relationships originating and developing in complex socio-economic systems, which grow in conditions of uncertainty and are accelerated by speculative contexts; moreover, they are characterized by irrational behaviours and give origin to stories. The Economy of trust plays a replacement function of guarantee in deregulated contexts and in situations of loss of institutional power.

The definition of 'Economy of Trust', which effectively illustrates current society and the global economy, contains the essence of Keynesian thought: this original notion highlights the idea of value tied to irrational trust relating to the marginal efficiency of capital; to investment demand; money markets; and assets capital. In this perspective, the definition of the economy of complexity is moreover justified by the involvement of the issues of uncertainty, speculation and stories embedded in this concept.

Furthermore, through this notion, the need for regulation arises against the vacuum of control, emblematic of the deregulated monetarist markets and in the absence of guarantees to protect against the uncertainty of the markets' fluctuations, and the possible resultant panic or euphoria.

Along these Keynesian theoretical premises, we are going to illustrate the concept of the Economy of Trust starting with a basic clarification which constitutes the first answer to the initial question 'Why does trust fall during crises?': the fact that we faced a drop in trust during the crisis' peak doesn't mean in any way that trust is lacking within the wider society: trust is an irrepressible energy as well as being the foundation of an individual's need for life. The individual *has a vital need* to trust.

Luhmann, in his systemic theory, brings the concept to its extreme consequences, arguing that if we didn't trust, we couldn't even wake up from bed in the morning (Luhmann, 2002). Specifically, the more the social system where trust originates is characterized by uncertainty, the more we need to rely on someone or something in the form of trust, confidence or 'rational trust' (see Chapter 2).

So, why are we discussing a drop in trust? If it is true that trust doesn't disappear, it is equally true that during the 2008 financial crisis, trust on those institutions in charge of being trustworthy to society plummeted, namely governmental institutions, the political class and those institutions in charge of preserving with respecting rules. In other words, it dropped right that institutional and systemic trust towards those institutions from which we expect the top trustworthiness due to norms, social contract, and shared culture. However, trust hasn't disappeared but it has been channelled towards other entities covering the new role of strong trustworthy powers (rating agencies, hedge fund companies, other financial institutions ...). After all, in a framework deregulated both in terms of the exchange process and ethical behaviour, market agents, including the ultimate individual who has bought, with no specific information, subprime mortgage bonds in the wake of an overheated market, have a strong *need to trust* the economic action they are going to undertake in order to match their economic objectives.

We are going to analyse below how this process of re-direction of trust takes place and what these new strong powers are.

In the goods and services exchange market, typical of a Nominal Economy, the pledge of the legitimacy of the value of the exchanged assets is operated mainly by trust. In fact, as trust doesn't require the validations or specifications of the exchange regulation, it facilitates the exchange process while reducing costs of transactions. Moreover, when the exchanged objects are of difficult measurability and comparison, trust plays a key role in the warranty of the exchange (Mutti, 1998, p. 51). This basic aspect of trust as a substitute for guarantee and control of institutions, already tackled in Chapter 2 through the issue of trust in the socio-economic systems, is of great relevance. It reflects the current absence of an institution that regulates global finance, or, probably more realistically, the absence of a normative global system coordinated by a network of institutions in charge of warranting the coverage of the major areas of the geo-political and virtual space involved in financial exchanges.

In substance, trust absorbs such a vacuum, by transforming it into different substitutive forms: its versatility, founded on the absence of ratifications, of agreements and contracts; and its speed and intangibility fully matching the requirements of the Nominal Economy where it operates.

A circumstance of void of institutional control, as that which occurred before and after the 2008 slump, for instance, has led groups and élites, skilled in establishing trustworthy relationships both peer-to-peer (trust agreements) and towards the buying market (buy-and-sell transactions), to conquer positions of power. We refer to financial companies, hedge funds and other financial institutions that had the ability to catalyse trust, launching great volumes of financial bonds onto the market. This led them to become fully co-responsible for the crisis that exploded. It

DOI: 10.1057/9781137467232.0006

is not even difficult to imagine the possible existence of control rooms placed within the virtual global network of financial markets.

This void of institutional control has not only been occupied by financial bodies of a corporate nature: there are entire nations which have acquired 'institutional financial' roles. We may think about China which, thanks to its double figure growth rates, is in the position to warrant the solvency of any credit and may provide loans high enough to fund an entire other nation. A case in point is the treasury debt position of the United States of America towards the 'Asian tiger'. These phenomena, from derivatives finance to loans between countries, indicate the severe difficulties in governing a multi-centric and diversified global financial system: the International Monetary Fund (IMF), the World Bank, the World Trade Organisation (WTO) or the Financial Stability Board (FSB) all constantly encounter this complex issue.

In this void of powers, financial companies, experts and rating agencies leverage their available information, their accesses to information and their expertise in filtering and validating the most profitable sources. They represent the 'new institutional powers' of the financial global network. Moreover, the position of power acquired by these 'intermediate bodies' has an autopoietic (self-generating) strength – that is, it self-feeds and self-adapts: the more high quality information they own, the more their credibility and their systemic power to grow in acquisitions is reinforced.

Never in our current post-modern age, in the context of a Nominal Economy summing up speculative features, absence of rules, and irrationality, has such a tight 'money – information – power' triangle been forged. Here, information as a crucial component of reputation, covers a paramount role. Information *is* money and money flows at the speed of information along the digital highways of real time. Information is power as it is the cause and effect of profit production and profit is the aim of these 'new institutions'. Indeed, they don't do anything but accomplish their institutional mission.

The dilemma is if the roles of democratic warranty of rights and equity are related to an institutional–government substitutive position. Unfortunately, the reality of the 'new institutions' appears to be far removed from this picture, contributing greatly to the generation of a deep climate of social uncertainty, need for trust, security and predictability.

Indeed, the more the social system within which trust takes origin is characterized by uncertainty, the more the need for trust arises. This

DOI: 10.1057/9781137467232.0006

need, as we have already seen, tied to the innate need for security or control within the socio-economic realm, finds its highest expression in the craving to predict. The issue of predictability and of the probability underlying predictability is a core Keynesian issue, tackled by the economist through the already mentioned 'Keynesian convention'.

If Adam Smith had been right and the functioning of the free market had led to the predicted unintentional consequences of a balanced distribution of wealth, the economic, social and ethical issues originated by the new strong powers during the 2008 crisis would not have arisen.

On the contrary, reality shows a different situation: the end of 2009 registered, at the global level, the highest amount of unemployment within the range of 15 to 24-year-old young people[3]: we are talking about 81 million young people, with a global increase of the youth unemployment rate from 2007 to 2009 from 11.9% to 13%; moreover, if we notice the increase in the unemployment rate of the European Union, within the same period, an increase of +2.2 percentage points, from 6.7% in March 2008 to 8.9% in May 2009[4] was registered; furthermore, the accountability of the 2008 downturn shows that US\$4.1 trillion had been pulverized, equalling £2.8 trillion: more than US\$630 of illusion of wealth 'for every man, woman and child on the earth'.[5] 'Pulverized' appears to be the correct term, since what is left behind initially by the financial slump, and after by the economic downturn, is a recession driving the entire world towards a new poverty and to a new redistribution of wealth affecting human lives. Let us think about incomes, jobs, housing, health care and social securities of the countries still fighting defaults.

Keynes was extremely worried about poverty. In his Moorian view, poverty relates to an idea not only of financial hardships but also of scarcity of wealth, of restrictions on the freedom of human action, of constraints on new idea development and the promotion of culture. War, bringing heavy burdens of costs, is seen by Keynes as being responsible for impoverishment on a grand scale. In 'The Economic Consequences of Peace', the Master reports that the compensation asked of Germany, following its defeat in the first World War, was so great as to place the German Government in default, thus bringing it to its knees, unable to benefit from or contribute to European post-war prosperity.

Diversely, the aim of the Keynes' plan on how to pay the costs of the war appears 'social', that is, aiming to prevent losses to persons and families caused by inflation 'according to a principle of social justice allowing

DOI: 10.1057/9781137467232.0006

adequate incentives to labour and economy' (Keynes 1971–89, XXII, p. 218; Skidelsky, 1996, p. 114).

During the period following the Second World War, Keynes relentlessly takes part, personally, in the negotiations of the American loan in favour of a Great Britain in great economic distress, having to settle an amount heavily lower than the objective, just to moderate the risks of inflation and unemployment, besides the issue of social order: inflation represents an issue, if not an impediment, to the redistribution of wealth.

Probably, the hypotheses presented by some scholars and experts in considering speculative bubbles as the new forms of global war and the hypotheses of a Third World War aren't so imaginative, judging by the levels of poverty that wide portions of the world population have experienced during the initial crisis and the recession that has followed.

Or, instead, it could be more correct to consider that we are in a phase of realignment over a past illusion of excessive prosperity, generated by a Nominal Economy that has created a misleading perception of wealth leading to greediness and deception.

What is certain is that behind this process, the factor 'trust' has governed many variables.

This is true also in light of another consideration: trust has no ethics, it is neutral. Trust may be built within a criminal organization as in a social entrepreneurship. Positive or negative outcomes of the effects of trust depend upon persons and aims, wills, intentions and values of subjects acting with a *sense*, as Weber would say. This means that the components of his construct as: competence, benevolence, integrity, transparency, identification or value congruence contain a feature of relativity, in the ethical sense. Within deceit, there may be competence; the leader of a criminal organization may certainly be benevolent and unselfish towards a member of the group. It is not necessary to be Benthamians[6] to understand how even altruism may be driven by a personal interest; a case in point is represented by companies becoming trustworthy to stakeholders via corporate social responsibility actions which are profit-driven rather than carried out for pure philanthropy; besides, integrity and transparency may be expressions of intrinsic coherence in pursuing unethical lucrative aims, not to mention the need for identification between members of a gangsters mob, for example.

These considerations allow us to understand how, in the current economic scenario, trust has operated according to what many complain

DOI: 10.1057/9781137467232.0006

about, being a drive led by greediness, deceit and corruption of ethical principles. After all, as already mentioned, the Nominal Economy is the economy of illusion, an economy that alters the perception of the real and which deceives.

However, there is a 'good' trust that exists. It is the trust that feeds hopes and encourages the growth of the economic system, nurturing expectations with positivity and allowing the economic policy programmes to turn into action in short times spans; that trust enables accelerated, exponential, positive results for a new government whilst empowering individuals according to principles of reciprocity and acknowledgement; it's a trust that, in essence, is tied to competence, benevolence, integrity, transparency and the identification of values. It is a 'trust belief' that aims to enhance ethically valuable thoughts and actions.

Keynes firmly believed in the 'good' trust because he trusted the strength of optimism and the intellectual qualities of the individual. He had a mainly positive vision of life and the future. We have mentioned in Chapter 1 how Keynes puts capitalism at the basis of the process of development only up to reaching a future of material and intellectual aesthetics.

Unfortunately, this 'good' trust may be misplaced. The reasons for the drop in the trust indicators during the financial slump have indicated causes traceable to a process of distrust towards national governments: from the Eurozone debt crisis to the corruption scandals in Brazil, and the aftermath management crisis of the 2011 earthquake in Japan. These disillusions just reduce governments' trustworthiness. Trust requires confirmations and if these fail, the circular process breaks up, shifting into distrust. As we have seen, in fact, trust binds the past to the future: it builds on the perception of past behaviour to project interaction in the future. If the past is marked by negative experiences, the future building will be more difficult.

There is an aspect, however, worth noting: we have talked about a 'perception' of behaviour. The behavioural economics teaches us that it's the frame of reference that influences perception – undoubtedly, the climate of uncertainty characterizing a socio-political situation as the current one influences judgements, media condition opinions and reputation. In particular, we have seen from the Edelman Trust Barometer how 'trust in media', the main informative source useful to make a judgement of reliability, has also plunged, reaching an all-time low level: as an ultimate effect, trust in the sources of trust, too, has dropped.

Here is the final consequence of a systemic collapse of the trust relationship, generating, in turn, further spirals of distrust – 'consumer

DOI: 10.1057/9781137467232.0006

security', 'higher regulation in business' and 'control of the big corporates' behaviour' – these are what people asked for in 2011, in the middle of the greatest economic downturn in history (Edelman Trust Barometer, 2011). In such a pervasive climate of uncertainty people require protection, seeking safety and security.

By acknowledging the institutional loss of the sovereign economic, political, social power, as is happening to the governments of the main authorities, a form of autonomous, individual, short-term government is engendered within the individual also. The subject, feeling distrust towards the government or the central institutions responsible for the functioning of finance, tends to look for safety within the socio-economic realm by selecting trustworthy entities in relation to conditions of tangibility. This means that he or she tends to identify those relationships which appear to be more controllable (as the interpersonal buyer-seller trust or peer-to-peer trust); otherwise, in a condition of higher verifiability of the trust beliefs and lower institutional complexity, the individual tends to 'focus' his or her expectations and motivations by adopting institutional and systemic trust to receive advice and indications. This trust could be towards rating agencies, financial companies, but also, in the social realm, social networks and virtual communities.

This pattern of self-management rising within the Economy of Trust, stemming from the absence of institutional reference points, such as the government, is extremely dangerous.

The single 'ignorant individual left to himself', as Keynes calls it, (Keynes, 2006, p. 340) doesn't enjoy enough information to compete with the standards of the 'expert professionals, possessing judgment and knowledge beyond that of the average private investor' (Keynes, 2006). Therefore, his or her actions are moreover subject to irrationality, to the Animal Spirits and to a process appearing more imitative than autonomous. It's an action conditioned by the influence of collective behaviour, originating fluctuations and economic cycles. These are feared by Keynes as is any other economist concerned about the balances of the system and seeking any effective way to preserve those balances.

There are five sociological reasons explaining how the Economy of Trust develops in the context of a Nominal Economy: uncertainty, irrationality, speculation, complexity and stories. Even though these dimensions appear to be intrinsically connected, one to the other, we will examine them separately to highlight the different sides of the concept which is focus of our discussion.

DOI: 10.1057/9781137467232.0006

This reflection prepares the ground for a general discussion carried out under the Keynesian perspective that may provide useful information to a positive evolution in the Economy of Trust.

We are going to examine the first element now.

Uncertainty

> The outstanding fact is the extreme precariousness of the basis of knowledge on which our estimates of prospective yield have to be made. Our knowledge of the factors that will govern the yield of an investment some years hence is usually very slight and often negligible. (Keynes, 2006, p. 335)

The Economy of Trust develops in a context of high uncertainty.

Keynes, as we have seen, maintains that the economy is built on a radical uncertainty. In an article in 1937 (Keynes, 1937), The Master argues that neither a consumption function, nor an investment multiplier exists; instead, it only exists in vague and uncertain knowledge, fluctuant states of trust and courage, fears and hopes, managed at best by strategies and conventions, which may indeed be swept away by new occurrences. Keynes, with these words, suggests that uncertainty belongs to humanity. However, as seen in Chapter 2, the Economist makes a distinction between the concept of uncertainty and risk: the concept of uncertainty of Keynes essentially relates to the incompleteness of information. The latter regards unknown probabilities and stems from the inability of subjects to solve situations with fact-based decisions; the Keynesian risk, instead, is tied to known probabilities, it is a subjective calculation and it is related to the human action. In other words: we may manage risk and being responsible for it; conversely, uncertainty, not being dependent on us, has to be suffered, by finding strategies for surviving with it.

Why does uncertainty arise?

As a whole book wouldn't be enough to provide an exhaustive answer to this question, here we just highlight the main features of its causes behind: uncertainty arises by a space–time shift inside society. The factorization of these two vectors of human action onto two separate levels, disconnected between them, dissolves the traditional reference coordinates of human action.

This makes the individual fall into an emotional state of absence of certainties and leads him or her to autonomously build new coordinates for each new context. This disruption of space–time balances has a historical backdrop, tracing back to the industrial revolutions and to the evolutionary outcome of progress reflected in the social and economic realm.[7]

> In circumstances of space–time disjunction, the Economy of Trust represents the building of value as a form of control of uncertainty.

Keynes maintains that in former times when the ownership and management of enterprises corresponded, the entrepreneurial activity represented a way of life and prospective profit wasn't the result of a precise calculation. Affairs were to be considered as a lottery, even though governed by the abilities and character of the managers, above or below the average. 'Some would fail and some would succeed. But even after the event *no one would know* whether the average results in terms of the sums invested had exceeded, equalled or fallen short of the prevailing rate of interest' (Keynes, 2006, p. 337). This system of investment, following the old-fashioned pattern, generated stability in market values and prospective profit. The time factor, in these circumstances, was quite expanded.

Diversely, with the separation between ownership and management and with the development of securities markets, Keynes argues, if on the one side investment is helped, on the other, a high instability is generated.[8] This phenomenon placed by the economist at the basis of the issue of expectations and probability is attributable to a space–time shift: if, in fact, it is true that there is an inability to obtain adequate information by the financial operators, as information generates in places spatially far from one another and the human being is not ubiquitous, it is also true that the time factor plays a relevant role: the Stock Exchange reevaluates in real time the value of investments and at any reevaluation, the investor has to revise his or her profit expectations.

The key issue, argues Keynes, is that this process influences the present, that is, the current rate of investments.

> For there is no sense in building up a new enterprise at a cost greater than that at which a similar existing enterprise can be purchased; whilst there is an inducement to spend on a new project what may seem an extravagant sum, if it can be floated off on the Stock Exchange at an immediate profit. (Keynes, 2006, p. 337)

The long-term expectation, on which our decisions are based 'does not solely depend, therefore, on the most probable forecast we can make. It

DOI: 10.1057/9781137467232.0006

also depends on the *confidence* with which we make this forecast – on how highly we rate the likelihood of our best forecast turning out quite wrong.' (Keynes, 2006, p. 334) It means that not only our expectation on probabilities on the future event has relevance but also how we trust our statement to be true.

From this statement it emerges how the Animal Spirits, through expectations, govern uncertainty: they give shape to a trust instinct that allows average forecasts to be constructed based on which the decision on the investment is made. This aspect highlights the tight relationship between time–value–good, translating it into the relationship between investment and time. By explaining the functioning at the base of the formulation of the estimates on expectations, Keynes, in fact, maintains that certain categories of investments are regulated, based on the convention, by the average expectations of the stock exchange investors, and built on an evaluation of the market based on the level of information present at that time. In these circumstances, the uncertainty the investor experiences refers to an effective change of news in the future. To dominate or control this uncertainty he will transform it into a calculated risk, by formulating his own estimate of the probability that it will take place. This is an effort to 'rationalize' a state of irrationality. Indeed, it directly relates to the other element of the construct of trust, that is, speculation.

At the end of all these considerations, these features explain how the Economy of Trust leads to a building of value through the probabilistic definition of risk, which is nothing but an illusion of rationalization.

Such a definition is subjective, as in a condition of stability of the convention security is linked to 'short periods' and to a continued series of them: news, in fact, changes constantly. The illusion to rationalize what is uncertain and the effort to account a perceived uncertainty generates in reality a state of precariousness. Ulrich Beck interprets it by concentrating the idea of imponderable and elusiveness within the concept of risk.

Irrationality

> The only thing we have to fear is fear itself. (Franklin D. Roosevelt, 1933)[9]

This issue will be examined as a completion to the discussion that took place in Chapter 2: we have already seen, in fact, how the Theory of

DOI: 10.1057/9781137467232.0006

Rational Choice, to which current monetarism aspires, is rooted in the classical thought of Adam Smith; we have also examined how according to it the subject acts rationally towards an instrumental end, that is, with the aim of maximizing an objective function in the presence of constraints. The utilitarian approach, founded on the maximization of benefits and minimization of costs is tied to an idea of the explanation of the social life via Weberian means–end rational action, and not only of the Behavioural Economics.

On the contrary, Keynes observes that not only does the individual within his or her economic behaviour have undeniable irrational features, but that these attitudes reflect on the collective economic behaviour and, therefore, also involve the social realm: behind the Animal Spirits, this dynamic generates fluctuations at the base of the economic cycles.

Keynes, thanks to two other elements, also justified the mainly irrational economic behaviour known as the 'weight of the argument' and the 'moral risk'. The first regards the amount of data based on which an evaluation of probability is made. Indeed, the evaluation involves the level of trust we have on our judgment: Skidelsky maintains that 'the distinction made by Keynes on the rationality of a judgment and the confidence that this judgment is rational plays a crucial role in the discussion of the psychology of the investment explained in the General Theory' (Skidelsky, 1996, p. 50). This allows us to understand how the perspective of the subjective trust is much more powerful within the individual cognition than a rational objective belief.

Hence, the Keynesian concept of probability is tied to a subjective perspective,[10] in contrast to the classical theory prevalent during the pre-Keynesian time that placed probability within the natural facts: for example, if the frequency of car accidents is one in every ten cars, then according to the classical theory, the probability of accidents happening is 10%. Frequency is an objective statistic notion and it represents the probability.

On Keynes' view, instead, 'the mind could "reduce" uncertainty to probability by sensing that some results are more or less probable than others, perceiving a relationship of probability between data (premises) and the conclusion of an argument. Such a perception defines a "level of belief" in the conclusion' (Skidelsky, 1996, p. 50).

This sensing frame ties probability 'to logical intuition, regarded by Keynes to be wider and more powerful than the logic of frequencies'.

DOI: 10.1057/9781137467232.0006

These concepts put Keynes strongly in opposition to the Rational Choice Theory. Such a theory, in fact, grounded on the system of relative frequencies, adopts the inductive method that the economist contrasts as it *a priori* implies a determination of a probability to happen.

In substance, in a Keynesian perspective, 'trusting trust' represents a key dynamic within decision-making behaviour.

The second assumption of 'moral risk' suggests that it is more rational to strive for a minor benefit whose achievement appears less probable than to strive for a higher one whose achievement appears less probable when the two actions have the same probabilistic ratio (Skidelsky, 1996, p. 50). This principle of Burkian[11] origin inspired the political philosophy of The Master according to which governments should aim to maximize happiness or the short-term utility rather than the long one. This is the pillar of the Keynesian decision-making assumption. Keynes maintains that a high weight and the absence of risk proportionally increases the appeal of the action to which they refer. Alongside this notion, the Treatise on Probability becomes the basis of the Keynesian theory on economic behaviour.

That said, this side of human irrationality has very deep effects on all the Economics of Trust: consumption, profitability, production and employment are all directly connected to the economic behavioural psychology. Within this process, trusting trust becomes an element of reassurance on the exactness of expectations that, for a principle of rationality are projected only within the short-term.

Speculation

In a Nominal Economy, trust is a founding pillar of economic behaviour in contexts of risk and speculative activities. Along these premises we are going to examine the mechanisms of the generation of trust and of the creation of value, which contribute to the generation of the Economy of Trust.

The conceptual link between the idea of speculation and risk is centred on the forecast of future events, specifically, on the relationship between past, present and future. Indeed, the foundation of a trust action lies within the projection of the present on the future in terms of expectations and in the anticipation of the future to the present through forecasts.

DOI: 10.1057/9781137467232.0006

All these elements are taken into consideration in the definition of speculation by Kaldor:

> Speculation may be defined as the purchase (or sale) of goods with a view to resale (re-purchase) at a later date, where the motive behind such action is the expectation of a change in the relevant prices relatively to the ruling price and not a gain accruing through their use, or any kind of transformation effected in them, or their transfer between markets. (Kaldor, 1939, p. 1).

Based on this definition it is clear how the Nominal Economy is related to speculation by the projection to the future, while in the real economy, value is mainly built on the use of assets or on any process of transformation.

Yet Keynes explains that the concept of speculation also lies within the process of investment typical of a situation of real economy: the starting point is represented by the time lag between the financial disbursement and the achievement of financial gains; in this time lag, to the extent of paying wages and covering production expenditures, a debt position is generated; to such a position it may correspond to an expectation of earning, if there is confidence that prices will rise; or an expectation of losses in case a drop in prices occurs (Keynes, 2006, p. 114). We could define this circumstance as a 'natural speculation' generated by the mechanism of the investment.

In the financial economy, however, investments are related to speculation within the psychology of the Stock Exchange that multiplies its effects: 'When the majority of the investors will be confident in a rise of prices a boom will take place; when, instead, there is a generalized distrust, the instinct will be bearish and a situation of depression of the stock market will take place' (Skidelsky, 1996, p. 81). When, as in this case, the term 'speculation' ties to an attitude related to the psychology of mass expectations, subject to emotional trust impulses, it may be compared to 'gambling'.

There is, indeed, a relevant distinction between the speculator, that is the one acting along the principle of the comparison between risk and expected yields, and the gambler, betting for the sake of risk, accepting also the possibility that the yield's expectation doesn't balance with the risk.

This distinction raises the issues of the social function and ethics within economic behaviour: the social judgement splits between supporters and opponents.

DOI: 10.1057/9781137467232.0006

Max Weber, in an essay of 1894, exalts the indispensable function of the Stock Exchange in the transmission of the economic process and the role of speculation as the engine of the stock exchange. Speculation allows information on price risks to be transmitted, thereby fulfilling their function of insurance. This is based on the ability to balance expectations with the transmission of information throughout the market. Alberto Beneduce[12] (Beneduce, 1915, p. 93) argues that speculation, through the insurance mechanism, safeguards price stability. This function is useful to the social life similarly to other forms of production of wealth. Speculation leads to an improvement in the professional abilities of the investors, expelling from the market the less capable speculators. Besides, following the law of demand and offer, it temporally coordinates the offer by balancing purchases with sales inversely to the availability of goods.

Keynes shows himself to be particularly worried for the consequences of the financial economy of his time, responsible for market fluctuations. This critique, which excludes all forms of speculation, relative to any real economy or entrepreneurial processes of investment, refers to the uncontrolled functioning of the Stock Exchange.

It is worth being reminded that any strong fluctuation corresponds to a disruption of the social order, causing masses of people being swept away from the job market, thus contributing to the well-known picture of long queues of unemployed.

As we will illustrate in the next paragraph on complexity, professional speculators, in fact, don't act according to autonomous expectations but they rather follow the psychology of the prevalent choices of the masses.

Keynes, therefore, considers speculation to be the *activity of forecasting the psychology of the market*, while entrepreneurship is the activity aiming to predict the prospective yields of capital assets for the duration of their life.

It is certain how speculation not always predominates over entrepreneurship, but the more markets are organized, the more the risk of the predominance of the first over the latter taking place. In fact, in a market characterized by a 'specialization of the function' Keynes explains how the economy of production or 'real' economy leads to a natural mechanism of speculation and how such a mechanism becomes 'institutionalized' as part of the suffered risk which is taken on by professional speculators (Keynes, 2006, p. 114).

It is easy to imagine how a radicalization of the organizational levels of the market leads professionals to excessive speculative behaviour.

DOI: 10.1057/9781137467232.0006

Also Pareto made a distinction between speculators and *rentiers* (asset owners), indicating the first as 'living investors on variable incomes' and the second as 'living savers on a fixed income' by counterposing the impulse towards the economic drive to the tendency for stability (Pareto, 1911, pp. 157–66).

Besides these remarkable reflections, it is evident how any form of pathology of speculation appears extremely dangerous to the social balance, to social cohesiveness and societal wellbeing. Excessive speculation generates an ill economy, with deceit built on ethical asymmetries, manipulation or unlawful uses of information, institutionalized hoarding and fraud. All of these damage the single unwary and inexperienced investor.

In the financial market, in fact, there are two categories of subjects, spaced out by a different level of cognition, experience and information: on one level, there is the restricted circle of professional investors and expert speculators, enjoying high levels of cognition and assessment ability; on the other, the private investors and single individuals lacking information and support. The professional investors build profits in the short time by 'foreseeing changes in the conventional basis of valuation a short time ahead of the general public' (Keynes, 2006, p. 341). In this perspective, the main interest of the professional is in the forecast of those events that may influence the collective market psychology. This kind of investment market, one that aiming to attack 'liquidity', appears to be highly antisocial: we refer to the lack of protection towards the single investor as, in the sharing of norms and values the financial market investors should subordinate the individual interest in favour of the group (Fukuyama, 1996, p. 23; Putnam, 1993). In other words, this process pulverizes that effect of acceleration of positive creation of social capital carried out by the 'store of value' produced by trust.

Keynes highlights this social stance, foreseeing an acceleration of the trend in this direction up to nowadays and stating that: 'The social object of skilled investment should be to defeat the dark forces of time and ignorance which envelop our future. The actual, private object of the most skilled investment to-day is "to beat the gun", ... to outwit the crowd, and to pass the bad, or depreciating, half-crown to the other fellow.' (Keynes, 2006, p. 341).

The Master compares it to a war of cunning between those succeeding in guessing the conventional short-term basis instead of ensuring a perspective yield out of a long-term investment, as stated by the real

DOI: 10.1057/9781137467232.0006

economy principles, anchored to production. This game among investors may resemble the game of musical chairs: there's always someone left without a seat when the music stops. Keynes maintains that speculators, individually, wouldn't cause any social damage 'as bubbles on a steady stream of enterprise. But the position is serious when enterprise becomes the bubble on a whirlpool of speculation. When the capital development of a country becomes a by-product of the activities of a casino, the job is likely to be ill-done.' (Keynes, 2006, p. 345).

Here, Keynes assimilates financial market speculation to gambling, and as such, considers it as leading to an irresponsible attitude, endangering the health of society and the economy.

Hence, the Stock Exchange, in its role of 'liquid' investment market, strongly calls for a regulatory function of institutions (Keynes, 2006, p. 346). Wall Street, according to Keynes, 'regarded as an institution of which the proper social purpose is to direct new investment into the most profitable channels in terms of future yield, cannot be claimed as one of the outstanding triumphs of *laissez-faire* capitalism — which is not surprising, if I am right in thinking that the best brains of Wall Street have been in fact directed towards a different object.' (Keynes, 2006, p. 345).

It was the great slump of 1929.

From the above considerations, which have certainly not exhausted such a complex topic, it emerges how speculation plays a role within the Economy of Trust as a bond between present and future. This aspect of the Nominal Economy that we are going to tackle in the next chapter relates to unethical actions calling for regulations to protect the weakest subjects.

Complexity

> We have reached the third degree where we devote our intelligences to anticipating what average opinion expects the average opinion to be. (Keynes, 2006, p. 342)

In the first chapter we acknowledged Keynes as the Economist of Complexity, thanks to the subtle ability of the Master to grasp the relevance of the context within which economic decisions are taken. This term also refers to the criss-crossing of expectations within the market

DOI: 10.1057/9781137467232.0006

actors at the base of the Keynesian convention. The understanding of the market psychology becomes, therefore, the strategic basis of economic behaviour: similarly to the protagonist of the movie 'A Beautiful Mind', where Russell Crowe's character, by applying the Theorem of the Nash equilibrium (Nash, 1951) to win a girl's love, enhances his strategy by matching the hypotheses of optimization of the other players, or, similarly to the chess strategies, Keynes explains the decision-making mechanism based on the expectations of the others' behaviour.

In the General Theory, the Economist illustrates the case of newspapers competitions 'in which the competitors have to pick out the six prettiest faces from a hundred photographs, the prize being awarded to the competitor whose choice most nearly corresponds to the average preferences of the competitors as a whole; so that each competitor has to pick, not those faces which he himself finds prettiest, but those which he thinks likeliest to catch the fancy of the other competitors, all of whom are looking at the problem from the same point of view' (Keynes, 2006, p. 342).

In this way Keynes relates the decision (which face will win) inside a context (which will be the average opinion). This implicitly means that the real talent is not in the ability of judgement but in the psychological investigative attitude of other persons.

The Game Theory, within which the Nash Theorem represents a step ahead in the uncooperative games, can predict the effects of possible actions based on the understanding of the rational assumptions behind each players' decision.[13] Keynes reaches the same outcome with a mixture of rationality and intuition: rationality to pinpoint the average of the evaluations of the other competitors on which face will be judged as the prettiest, and intuition on the possible psychological behaviour of the public. This will lead to the definition of a probable social behaviour.

Besides, the trust factor influences the assessment of the other people's behaviour, thus impacting on the level of confidence in the exactness of that choice. This process represents a more complex approach, rich in psychological implications that put the rational interpretation of the Theory of Games in a more complex light, similar to a game of poker or bridge.

Keynes has always placed importance on intuition and psychological analysis, considering them a form of talent essential to achieve success. Thanks to these qualities it is possible to analyse the emotional context of a fact: the Keynesian convention is based just on these considerations.

DOI: 10.1057/9781137467232.0006

The analysis of collective psychology, however, is quite complex as, being different from assumptions of individual rationality, it eludes the linearity of rational behaviour, instead requiring talented leaps of intuition.

As the Arrow theorem (Arrow, 1951) explains, individual preferences don't aggregate in a structure of collective preferences following the same individual assumptions. Therefore, within a group's behaviour, rules distant from the maximization of preferences, may emerge (Barry and Hardin, 1982). Stakeholders, in fact protagonists of the economic setting, behave according to the laws of the crowd, that is, the so-called lower orders of people in general or of a mob, gathered in a real or virtual place.[14]

The crowd sets up forms of collective action that are often irrational, such as the panic triggered through the viral mechanism of contagion. The 'circular reaction', in fact, determined by the response of many individuals to the same stimulus, reinforces the common behaviour. The collective behaviour tends to suspend usual behaviours and attitudes, making relationships more fluid, spontaneous and engaging, that is, emotional; the corresponding social personality of the individual, constituted by the set of his or her roles, tends to be suspended. For instance, the rational assumptions used for a specific calculation of the expected yields on a security investment, tends to be overcome against a crowd of investors suddenly selling that security. This triggers an unpredictable, erratic, imitative attitude that may be totally irrational, which may bring a behaviour opposed to the initial assumptions (Smelser, 1969).

In conclusion, in a complex and systemic condition such as the global one, the Economy of Trust is influenced by the irrationality within the collective psychological behaviour. This helps to determine robust forecasts extremely difficult.

Stories

A story is a tool used to provide an interpretation and an understanding of a reality, characterized by a succession of facts with an internal logic and dynamic. It allows the individual to confer sense and meaning to his or her experience (Bruner, 1988; Bruner, 1991, pp. 17–18): our actions follow a narrative route, as the narration provides a functional use of

DOI: 10.1057/9781137467232.0006

our action in a specific socio-cultural context. Otherwise, it would be an unconnected set of events and facts, lacking sense and relationship.

Trust is also a story, a chain of perceptions and actions linked together, whose essence is qualitative, through not being quantifiable. As the economic mainstream tends not to give credit to qualitative elements, essentially relying on quantitative data, the story helps quite clearly to explain the functioning of markets (Akerlof and Shiller, 2009, p. 84): the sequence of facts becomes therefore the basis on which the individual's economic behaviour is formulated.

Often, these behaviours are not quantitative elements, but just opinions, rumours, that are a *sum* of judgements influencing in turn other attitudes in an interlinked series of behaviours.

Stories are indifferent to the reliability of information: content that is transmitted may be real or false at the same time. Even stories founded on false arguments follow the logic of the *self-fulfilling prophecy*, a definition coined by Merton (Merton, 1968, p. 477), becoming trustworthy narrations. The self-fulfilling prophecy is a self-generating and self-feeding prediction, based on a positive feedback mechanism between belief and behaviour. The latter, becoming the validation of the correctness of the belief and the course of the facts, confirms that belief. Such a process appears clear in the bull or bear phases of the Stock Exchange, where the act of selling feeds the idea that the value of the securities is decreasing.

The character of this course of action projects through to future expectations. Trust built along different circumstances, therefore, doesn't represent an emotional state of the individual, but it rather becomes a 'trust of trust', that is, relying on the opinion of others based on trust on other subjects' perception, and so on. It turns out to be a true vision of the world, not founded on quantitative facts as biased by perceptions; it is a mode of reworking information on a reputation based on information provided by media and 'buzz' among people.

Positive stories propagate as epidemics, via word of mouth, 'heating' the economy which reacts with an inflationary trend (when the tendency is to buy), nurturing trust in purchases: the one who trusts, purchases, the one not trusting, stays at home and sells.

Stories best passed into history are the ones leveraging the imaginary of people, the dream of earnings: the euphoria of an easy accumulation of wealth has forerun the burst of any speculative bubble in the history of time, from the Tulip bubble in the first half of the seventeenth century to the 2008 speculative bubble of the subprime mortgage crisis.

DOI: 10.1057/9781137467232.0006

The subsequent slumps, however, easily destroy illusions.

The spread of stories is often helped by a process of synthesis of information, condensed in simple but effective pictures: just as the long queues of unemployed at the employment counters have become the black and white symbols of the 1929 Great Slump; and Tahir Square, crowded with protesters has become the symbol of the Arab Spring. These are pictures that in the Economy of Trust work as mediators to help the understanding (Dilthey, 1949; Weber, 1968) of meaningful relationships among signs (Boudon, 1970, p. 22). Used to nourish global stories, they are ultimate iconographic vehicles of the loss or gain of trust.

In conclusion, this third chapter has been devoted to the identification of answers regarding the reasons why, during the financial crisis of 2008, trust towards institutions has dropped, and what the consequences were.

In such a framework, the concept of Economy of Trust has acquired a definite shape, helping us to state some elements synthesized below in three points:

1 Trust has not disappeared, rather it has been channelled differently. By playing a substitutive role of guarantee it has spontaneously turned its direction from the traditional institutions to the new strong powers (rating agencies, hedge funds, financial corporates).
2 The global condition of uncertainty has favoured the acceleration of speculative phenomena, supported by mass psychology, stories, illusions and Keynesian irrationality.
3 The unfeasibility of a rational forecast, the law deregulation not protecting the weakest people has prevented a rational and calculated management of risk, damaging many categories of subjects.

As seen in the above three points, the Economy of Trust, therefore, has produced value, wealth, but with no equity, which is a building block of the process of development. This topic leads us to the last chapter.

Notes

1   Edelman Trust Barometer, Annual Global Opinion Leaders Study 2011. Answers using a 9-point scale where 1 means that 'you do not trust them at all' and 9 means you 'trust them a great deal'. Informed publics aged 25–64

DOI: 10.1057/9781137467232.0006

in 20 country global total. Available at www.Trust.edelman.com, accessed 20 December 2011.

2   Dizionario Etimologico. Available at http://www.etimo.it/?term=economia, accessed 15 June 2014.

3   ILO Global Employment Trends for Youth 2010. Available at http://www.ilo.org/wcm-sp5, accessed 20 September 2011.

4   Eurostat data. Available at http://www.epp.eurostat.ec.europa.eu, accessed 16 October 2011.

5   IMF data. Available at http://www.imf.org, accessed 24 November 2011.

6   Jeremy Bentham was an English utilitarian philosopher and social reformer. Bentham's campaign for social and political reforms in all areas, most notably criminal law, had its theoretical basis in his utilitarianism, expounded in his *Introduction to the Principles of Morals and Legislation*, a work written in 1780 but not published until 1789. In it he formulated the principle of utility, which approves of an action insofar as an action has an overall tendency to promote the greatest amount of happiness. Happiness is identified with pleasure and the absence of pain. To work out the overall tendency of an action, Bentham sketched a felicific ('happiness-making') calculus, which takes into account the intensity, duration, likelihood, extent, etc. of pleasures and pains. Available at http://www.utilitarianism.com/bentham.htm, accessed 3 July 2014.

7   The uncertainty characterizing the post-modern age is attributable to a social process started with the first industrial revolution of the early eighteenth century, by the rise of modern capitalism. This action of space–time disruption starts with the separation of work from the domestic household (Weber, 1968) engendered by factory work. The twentieth century of 'great differentiation and disembedment' (Bauman, 2003, p. 28) sees the splitting of producers from their livelihood (K. Marx, K. Polanyi). Such a disjunction produces two effects: the rise of profit and 'the simultaneous disjunction of human livelihood from the network of moral, emotional, family and neighbourhood bonds' (Bauman, 2003, p. 29), which simultaneously are emptied of all the meanings they had in the past. The space–time displacement accelerated by the digital revolution has contributed to separating the flux of information from the body motion (Bauman, 2003, p. 14). Many sociologists have tackled this issue, from M.A. Giddens to N. Luhmann, F. Lyotard to M. Castells and M. McLuhan under the technological perspective.

8   In the absence of security markets, there is no object in frequently attempting to revalue an investment to which we are committed. But the Stock Exchange revalues many investments every day and the revaluations give a frequent opportunity to the individual (though not to the community as a whole) to revise his commitments [...]. But the daily revaluations of

the Stock Exchange, though they are primarily made to facilitate transfers of old investments between one individual and another, inevitably exert a decisive influence on the rate of current investment. For there is no sense in building up a new enterprise at a cost greater than that at which a similar existing enterprise can be purchased; whilst there is an inducement to spend on a new project what may seem an extravagant sum, if it can be floated off on the Stock Exchange at an immediate profit.Thus certain classes of investment are governed by the average expectation of those who deal on the Stock Exchange as revealed in the price of shares, rather than by the genuine expectations of the professional entrepreneur. (Keynes, 2006, p. 338)

9   The first inauguration of Franklin D. Roosevelt as the 32nd President of the United States was held on Saturday, 4 March 1933. The inauguration marked the commencement of the first four-year term of Franklin D. Roosevelt as President and John Nance Garner as Vice President. Available at: www.whitehouse.gov, accessed 22 June 2014.

10 Anna Carabelli (Carabelli, 1988) defines it as a 'logic of the opinion'.

11 Edmund Burke, author of *Reflections on the Revolution in France*, is known to a wide public as a classic political thinker. All his life Burke retained a sense of the responsibility of the educated, rich and powerful to improve the lot of those whom they directed; a sense that existing arrangements were valuable insofar as they were the necessary preconditions for improvement; and a strong sense of the importance of educated people as agents for constructive change, change which he often contrasted with the use of force, whether as method or as result. Available at http://www.plato.stanford.edu, accessed 7 July 2014.

12 Alberto Beneduce (1877–944) was an Italian economist and politician promoting a socially oriented idea of reforms of state intervention.

13 The explanation of the note on the 'Prisoner's dilemma' in Chapter 2, the paragraph on Pre-Keynesian Economy.

14 'Occupy Wall Street' is a case of collective behaviour. The mob, virtually gathered and transposed in the reality of the mob occupations of Zuccotti Park in New York, has virally diffused in other parts of the world (Le Bon, 2004).

DOI: 10.1057/9781137467232.0006

4
Trust, Growth, Development

Abstract: *This last chapter examines the role of trust within the socio-economic process of development. The chapter attempts to outline the relationship between the Economy of Trust and the socio-economic context, evidencing the synergies. By these premises, Padua examines how trust may relate to the concept of development, equity and redistribution, in light of the Keynesian process of 'civilization'.*

To this extent, the difference between the concept of growth and development, the concept of redistribution, equity and trust in Keynesian thought, and the concept of the economy of development related to the civilization process advocated by Keynes are examined. From these considerations, it emerges quite clearly how Keynesian trust represents the basic fabric of the social capital of a nation.

Keywords: equity and trust; growth and development; Keynesian civilization; redistribution; social capital

Padua, Donatella. *John Maynard Keynes and the Economy of Trust: The Relevance of the Keynesian Social Thought in a Global Society*. Basingstoke: Palgrave Macmillan, 2014. DOI: 10.1057/9781137467232.0007.

This last chapter tackles the role of trust within socio-economic development.

This chapter attempts to briefly outline the relationship between the Economy of Trust and the context of global socio-economic development, highlighting the factors of synergy.

With these premises our attempt is to understand how trust may relate to the concept of development, equity and redistribution in the perspective of the Keynesian 'civilization' process.

Growth and development

The topic of development takes shape within economic and sociologic scientific thought,[1] starting with the post-war period along the dissolution of the colonial empires, on the one side, and the start of the bipolar tensions between the USA and the USSR on the other. The term *development*, concerning the achievement of both an economic and social progress finds its raison d'être in relation to its opposite, the notion of *underdevelopment*. This notion, implying low levels of productivity, economic stagnation and poverty, represents a starting point typical of the undeveloped or developing countries. The notion of development is associated with the notion of *economic growth*. This concept measures the economic expansion of a country, that is, the wealth produced by goods and services (Blanchard et al., 2011). It represents, though, a necessary but not sufficient condition to the achievement of development. While economic growth regards the satisfaction of the primary needs of the individual as feeding, health and housing, development represents a form of progress coupling the economic side to the social perspective. Indeed, to the achievement of the primary conditions, development together with the respect of basic human rights allow to achieve the primary conditions as access to education, civil freedom and political participation.

In the twenty-first century, development and growth has disrupted the nineteenth century geo-political balances: the rise of new, strong economies combined with the recession in historically dominant regions appears to design a multi-centric geography of power. In such a context, the barycentre of the production of wealth appears, moreover, to have shifted from west to east, overcoming the Bretton Woods political balances.

DOI: 10.1057/9781137467232.0007

Nowadays, the traditionally developed countries have to face many challenges: long-term crises of public balances heavily affected by welfare costs impacting on deficits; high debt dependency; shrinkage of available resources; a crisis of growth; and long-term structural unemployment. Essentially, we are not just in a phase of economic stagnation but of social, moral and trust arrest; of substantial loss of the value of work and hope; of the sense of equity and justice; and of social exclusion. While in western countries we are suffering the consequences of economic and mental wellness due to post-war progress and welfare is subject to political consensus, nowadays, the fragmented and individualized global society shows not to have new stimula but only personal interest. This aspect mirrors the widespread social indifference towards the unequal distribution of wealth, both at a national and a global level. Such a phenomenon of economic and social divergence, started during the 1970s, traces back to several reasons.

A first cause has to be traced back to a weakening or loss of central powers. Such a depletion of the powers of central governments reflects a lack of regulation, designed to govern sectors connecting entire geopolitical and economic regions, and offering warranties on the correct progress of the economic processes.

Second, the unequal distribution of wealth is impacted by deregulated markets: we have seen how Adam Smith's concept of the 'invisible hand' proved to be a pure illusion.

Third, the incompetence of politics to identify and implement new models of global governance denounces a heavy strain in managing the asymmetry between national interests and global markets.

Finally, developing countries such as China, India, and to a lesser or different extent, Brazil and Russia, are strongly emerging in the global scenario, altering the geography of wealth distribution. This process is taking place behind a drive to mend wide gaps in education, technology and innovation.

These factors impact the global economic power relationships established during the industrial revolution and during the rise of capitalism. Michael Spence, awarded the Nobel Prize for Economy in 2001, maintains that a 'divergence era' was originated during the post-war period where 15% of the population had reached wealthy status, leaving the remaining 85% in poverty; nowadays we may argue that we have entered an 'era of convergence': a good amount of the 85% of the world excluded by the processes of wealth growth and production is enjoying a positive chance to emerge in the international economic scenario.

DOI: 10.1057/9781137467232.0007

From the twentieth century geo-political setting, throughout the bipolar system following the Second World War, followed by the collapse of the Berlin wall in 1989, the global order setting, due also to the processes of globalization, has evolved to reach a polycentric fragmented layout. At the same time, countries are moreover interlinked and integrated, as Durkheim would argue.[2]

In this new picture, characterized by the Eurozone crisis, growth estimates project a different forecast from the current. Research by the Economist Intelligence Unit, Asian Development Bank, and International Monetary Fund (IMF),[3] projects that given that the global GNP is 100, in 2050 Asia may grow from the 22.5% of 2010 to 54% of the world GNP thanks to the presence of China and India; moreover, it estimates Europe to drop from 34% to 18% and North America to plummet from 31.5% to 15%; with South America projected to register lower growth, from 6.5% to 10%.

In the face of this growth and decline, the socio-economic scenario becomes possibly dark for many countries used to high standards of living: we ask ourselves, then, if some principles of the western order founded on a capitalistic economy and on liberal democracy may yet be credible?

Fukuyama maintains that the capitalistic-liberal model is still the reference model at the global level. This statement would be proved by the absence of a remarkable social reaction of contrast, apart from some phenomena such as the Indignados,[4] considered by Fukuyama of minor relevance (Farina, 2011, pp. 10–11). Fukuyama considers as viable a global convergence towards a liberal-democratic model of 'market-oriented economies and [considers realistic] an integration within the global labour division' (Fukuyama, 1996, p. 15).

Keynes also give a key role of growth to the capitalistic model – however on the condition of the presence of a leading role within the economy. This need of a regulatory role appears to be invoked in the Eurozone. Now some steps have, apparently, been taken by the European Central Bank (ECB).[5] However, only an ECB with full powers, may ensure those credit conditions as a guarantee of stability.

In Keynes, the topic of stability, tied to the role of the central government is positioned within the conceptual framework of 'socialization'. In Keynes, the issue of socialization is quite delicate, as this term hides behind the harshest critics of a model ('deficit spending') considered responsible for a public indebtment of which the effects are still tangible.

DOI: 10.1057/9781137467232.0007

The Keynesian 'Social State', if on the development side it has generated the trend of thought towards the 'Keynesianism of growth', with positive acknowledgements by the scientific community,[6] on the welfare programmes side it is common opinion that it has been ideologized. In fact, it appears to have been interpreted as the use of public spending as a tool to build consensus, free from the requirements of the economy tied to the level of unemployment and from the economic cycle phase (Trigilia, 1998, p. 97). It is easy to guess how this theory has become the symbol of government economic inefficiency and inability to manage the country's public budget and, as a consequence, responsible for high inflationary drives.

However, it is still true that the massive growth of the welfare policies following the consolidation of the socialization of the economy, is tied to a progressive legitimation of modern capitalistic democracies (Habermas, 1975). In fact, the growth of social protection programmes leads to the growing acknowledgement of civil, political rights and thus also of the social rights of the lower classes (Marshall, 1976; Bendix, 1964).

This, of course, also leads to a socio-political statement regarding an equitable access to educational institutions (Trigilia, 1998, p. 100).

For these reasons the welfare model is also placed within an idea of development, preserving the principles of equity, redistribution, protection from risks related to diseases, incidents, ageing and unemployment.

However, the applicability of the concept of individual governments leading their economies assumes a meaning inside the boundaries of the European Union; in the current global socio-economic scenario it appears to clash with strong asymmetries determined by some factors, not too relevant during Keynes' time – it deals with the relationship between techno-science and economic dynamics in favour of a technology appearing to have taken a leading role inside the countries' economies by coordinating them inside the global context.

The relationship between techno-science, a capitalistic economy and politics, represents a core problem not easy to solve, when placed within the context of growth and development. Fukuyama argues that in this phase of convergence, governmental institutions are no longer in the position to govern society via social engineering. The levels of global unemployment is a case in point, as the interlinking of the issues at the origin of the problem doesn't allow a solution on a local or national basis. Therefore, we are facing a massive danger (Severino, 2011): the risk that social issues are managed not in an economic-political mainframe but

DOI: 10.1057/9781137467232.0007

through a techno-scientific process. The 2008 crisis is an example, where the uncontrolled rise of finance on a technological and digital basis has channelled wealth into the hands of the few while the many had massive losses, widening a gap that would appear destined to further increase.

In light of the redistribution of global growth trends and a rise in the techno-economy, it is worth questioning whether we are experiencing a significant shift in the economic balance towards an increase in poverty, as some maintain (Pansa, 2011).

We have seen how Keynes was worried about the problem of a new poverty and how this fear wasn't just connected to an economic dimension but also a social and ethical one. This worry reflects the central role given to the issue of employment in the role of social cohesiveness.

In an interlinked context, a new matter and one of not minor relevance, is the merging of economic and social issues. We ought to ask ourselves what is the basis on which a possible growth of the western countries, currently living in a crisis of stagnation, can be measured? If, in fact, in absolute terms, a rise of the GNP becomes an incontrovertible datum, in relative terms how may we talk about growth on a real economy basis when the base calculation is inflated by a virtual indebtedness, as a result of a Nominal Economy? A case in point is the United States economy before the 2008 crisis.

Based on the above considerations, in the recent economic recession, the achievement of such an aim of social cohesiveness appears more complex. Postmodern society, in fact, not only has been affected by massive impacts on employment but it also suffers from endemic issues tied to a progressive individualism, to the disruption of ethical and democratic values, to increased social differentiation and to the disappearance of the middle class.

Due to the process of globalization, we have witnessed a phenomenon of 'social dumping' coupled to a law dumping (Vegas, 2012, p. 42): the less attractive law systems, not to lose their status, level their value system at the one adopted in the most competitive countries; as a consequence, the workers' wages are not related to a large extent to the cost of living of the specific country but rather to the comparative evaluation of the labour cost to the most efficient systems. The fallout is severe: if the middle class disappears, the savings traditionally generated by it also vanish. Consequently, investments shrink and that region weakens.

This last factor is largely responsible for the new forms of poverty related to global balances and it is bound to the distortions of the income system triggered by the disruption of the credit system of many western countries. Globalization, fiscal reforms and technological revolution, have all contributed to a widening between the wealthy social classes and the poor ones, realizing a progressive impoverishment of the middle classes.

In substance, we might witness a possible fading of capitalism in its traditional meaning, in favour of a progressive establishment of a technological economy. This would mean that as the Keynesian risk of the unintentional is brought into play, unconsidered and uncontrollable consequences of capitalism might be restrained by rationality and the economic science.

At this point, we ask ourselves, where is the threshold of resistance of the western countries to such a progressive impoverishment that society perceives as a clear divorce between capitalism and democracy, that is, between economy and those values seriously compromised by the enormous wealth-building process symbolized by the collapse of Lehmann Brothers in October 2008?

This social polarization between new and old powers is at the basis of a deep mistrust towards the institutional systems showing to be impotent before the global market processes and unable to play that expected social role of balance and preservation of economic and social rights.

In substance, we are facing an elusion of positive expectations, which, as seen in the previous chapters represents an essential component of trust.

All these evolutions bring the topic of trust to the forefront within social life bonds and public opinion, particularly within the relationship between citizens and political institutions, in the sense of justice and equity and in the general perception of security.

In light of these considerations, we reflect on the move to tackle the redistribution of wealth and equity, which is a key issue within the social approach of Keynesian civilization.

Redistribution, equity, trust

In economics, the theory of exchange deals with the object of the exchange, with actors and the output generated in relation to the input. In sociology, instead, the principles of equity and iniquity are introduced within the notion of exchange in contexts such as society, family, institutions and friendship.

DOI: 10.1057/9781137467232.0007

This means that if the market works following the assumptions of the *commutative*[7] justice that lies at the base of the exchange relationships of giving and receiving, social cohesiveness is a responsibility of *distributive* and *social* justice.

The relevant aspect is that these two latter forms of justice are in turn useful for the correct functioning of the market: 'without internal forms of solidarity and reciprocal trust, the market can't fully dispatch its own economic function. Today, it's this trust that has come to lack' (Pope Benedetto XVI, 2009, p. 37). This aspect is tied to the inequality between the wealth of different countries: even if we are in the age of convergence there are still many countries which could be potentially involved in the exchange process, which suffer high levels of inequality, being exploited by other rich countries taking advantage of them. Resources and low-cost labour are typical sources of exploitation.

The functioning of the market logic appears, therefore, to avoid the pursuit of the common good for which the political community is responsible through the action of redistribution. However, the difficulty is that this logic suffers the asymmetry between political competence and economic space that these days is global.

Keynes assigned a high value to equity, grounding it in a strong sense of meritocracy. With this term, we refer to that sense of justice allowing each individual to freely perform his or her abilities and talent, applied according to the means owned by everyone.

In Keynesian thought, the 'right' of the individual prevails over the collective 'good', the same as a statement of a liberal principle on a communitarian assumption (Rawls, 1999).

As Skidelsky maintains: 'Keynes shifted the issue of justice from micro-economy to macro-economy. The injustice was transformed into an issue of uncertainty, justice a matter of bargaining predictability... In the Economist's social philosophy redistribution plays a minor role and only as part of the functioning of the macro-economic stabilization, not as a tool to achieve an ideal objective as equality' (Skidelsky, 1996, p. 56).

We may say that the principle of social justice is transferred into a fair redistribution of sacrifices among the different categories of workers (Keynes, 1971–89, IX, pp. 146–7).

However, by transposing the Keynes' thought in post-modernity we couldn't narrow down the discussion to an equitable redistribution of fiscal weight, but in light of the relevance of the topic of uncertainty, we enlarged it to the topic of *risk redistribution*, alongside the thought

DOI: 10.1057/9781137467232.0007

of Ulrich Beck: in a modern reflective society where the production of risk prevails on the production of wealth, risk management acquires an economic, social and political relevance. Such risks, in fact, produce new inequalities at a global level: between the Third World and industrial countries and among the same industrial countries (see the crisis of the Eurozone), risk is impacting the international law and order.

Just as the 'life of a blade of grass in the Bavarian forest depends ultimately on the execution and observance of international treaties' (Beck, 2000, p. 30), Wall Street depends upon the fluctuation of the Euro – With the growing production and distribution of what Ulrich Beck calls 'bads', that is, all kind of risks that are the result (like products) of the modernization process that enhances class inequalities. As a matter of fact, risks, much like wealth, are distributed unevenly in a population and will influence the quality of life. Wealth differentials enable the advantaged ones to minimize their risk exposure and intensify it for the disadvantaged ones (Beck, 2000, p. 46). In other words, a low wage corresponds to a low level of security and plenty of risks; instead, where wealth builds, security and absence of risk may be bought. This is the ultimate meaning of social global injustice: not only an unequal redistribution of wealth but inequality also in the redistribution of risks.

Considering all that has been discussed in the previous chapters about the Keynesian theory, as it is not viable to calculate the probability of an event; risk management cannot be conceived as a rational process. However, the State and international politics have to act as guarantors of a situation of stability with the aim of favouring a state of social justice. This allows first, prevention of economic fluctuations in a global interlinked context which, in turn, gives origin to situations where the weakest and the least protected are put into conditions where their dignity, their freedom, their rights and their 'capabilities' are lost,[8] Amartya Sen would say; second, that the state of credit is guaranteed, to preserve the institutional credit role of banks warranting the solvability of loans; and, finally, that the government becomes guarantor of the solvability of the loans in a state of trust able to promote the economic exercise of the commutative exchange.

However, in the current atomized society, we are experiencing a general weakening of all typologies of traditional trust, that is, the ones linked to the community, as Ferdinand Tönnies[9] argues: we don't mean just *institutional trust*, as we have already seen, but *interpersonal trust*, that is, trust towards the 'other one' and *systemic trust* as well, focused

DOI: 10.1057/9781137467232.0007

on transnational organizations responsible for granting processes as the economic one.

In reality, we are witnessing a relational gap between people and institutions appearing unable to keep promises and support common projects typical of the model of 'trust in development'.

While the issue of development is tied to a long-term perspective, politics nowadays appear oriented towards short-term solutions where results may be more productively played out as goods of exchange (Cesareo, 2009): an example is the issue of individual safety against micro-criminality.

In such a void of political–institutional power at the global as well as at the national level, the system produces high levels of uncertainty calling for new forms of security.

At an individual level, interpersonal trust is channelled in different forms. Research run by Gi Group in collaboration with Od&M Consulting, run in Italy, on the levels of trust (from July to September 2011) shows that the highest level of trust is towards the company where one works. The least is towards institutions (consistently with what we have seen in Chapter 3, 44 points versus 26 on a base of 100); besides, inside companies, executives' trust shows to be higher than workers' trust (46 vs 43), and young people's trust appears higher than any other age group.

How might these results be interpreted?

The sociologist Luhmann helps in justifying this trust behaviour: the individual tends to reduce complexity by limiting trust inside boundaries of controllability (institutional and systemic trust). In other words, a company is trustworthy when it leverages a sense of belonging, it is a tangible reality and is a source of safe wage (up to this certainty is real...). A company is a more controllable entity than a government institution or a political party that, as has been seen, suffers a compromised image; similarly, executives have more information than workers on which trust may be built, naturally, in an organizational and financially healthy situation; on the contrary, the workers, having less information on company performance, are more inclined to be affected by the general climate of distrust. The case of young people, instead, is explained with the instinctual and optimistic approach tied to a longer life-perspective bearing higher chances of a positive future. An adult, instead enjoying a level of information higher than a young given his or her past experience is rationally disenchanted with easy optimism.

DOI: 10.1057/9781137467232.0007

Going back to the topic of uncertainty where the mechanisms of social protection dissolve, it has to be highlighted that the horizontal relationship gains further relevance. It represents a new social capital that operates following free trust mechanisms, sometimes turned into forms of rational utility or altruistic action.

These new middle social organizations between people and institutions are represented by social networks as Occupy Wall Street or in various forms of sociality expressed online.

In such a scenario the point is to understand how to channel the economy of trust towards ends able to grant the protection of social values such as cohesion, social capital, equity and redistribution, matters not only dealing with economic development but also with rights and human dignity.

According to Keynes, these are failed values because of the disruption of social protection mechanisms.

The Keynesian 'civilization'

The contribution offered by Keynes on this ground is not limited to an economic policy model, as it embraces a cultural approach of real 'civilization' involving a 'combination of free individuals, regulated markets, collective needs, international regulation without hegemonies, friendly governments (not compassionate).'[10]

Such a wide vision leads Keynes to observe the enormous gap in the wealth of different nations (Akerlof and Shiller, 2009, p. 176): according to Keynes, income and wealth depend on the market freedom of that country, from the abilities of people, the country's geography, its past and present wars, its public and legal institutions, but also from the technological innovation and the differences in propensities to save among different countries. Employment and income distribution become the pillars of Keynesian reflections supported by the philosophical and social principles of the Moorian and Burkian doctrines, founded on the key premises of ethical sense and equity.

It is worth pointing out that Keynes is politically utilitarian. The Master has an optimistic and materialistic vision about social progress (Helburne, 1991, p. 51): the ethical aim per se has no place, as in politics there are specific objects that have to be defined and achieved. In pursuing such objectives duty is carried out as it represents the method of each individual.

DOI: 10.1057/9781137467232.0007

Keynes maintains that 'in social life duty is method' (Bateman-Davis, 1991, p. 51). Such a method is not mechanistic and rejects any abstraction and universalism on behalf of the particular and the contingent. The refusal of the objectivity of dogma in the classical theory, in favour of the cognitive limits typical of the individual's knowledge, highlights how the concept of duty reinforces the position of antithesis towards the neoclassical economists.

At a macro level, the Keynesian civilization works with the aim of achieving desirable social objectives through the economy of development or the study of economic growth in poor countries, by a self-supported development model.

This principle is close to the idea of capabilities proposed by Amartya Sen. The comparison leads us to reflect how Keynes believes in merit, in equity conceived as equal opportunities, and in the equality of the starting positions; likewise, Sen's, 'capabilities' regard the set of the real opportunities that the State has to offer in providing the individual with the possibility to express his or her own ability to do and to be, granting the set of real opportunities a person has to realize a behaviour within his or her own life. Actually, it is an intrinsic act of trust in human qualities.

How can trust reinforce the process of civilization under a social perspective?

While in economics, exchange is evaluated in terms of money value, in sociology, the inputs or the social action and the outputs or feedback reactions to an action are evaluated in relation to a subjective value perspective (Blau 1964): even gratitude and thanking or the reaction to the presence or absence of sanction will be part of a balanced calculation, on a subjective basis, of the inputs versus the outputs of the exchange. In such a game, a sense of duty is involved to balance the two processes: people are happy when they may behave as they 'should behave'. This, for instance is the social meaning of duty inside the system of micro-credit designed by Muhammad Yunus,[11] whose success is determined by the sympathetic responsibility of the debtors against the loan reimbursement.

Under this perspective the Keynesian civilization implies, according to Fukuyama, that stability and prosperity are based not only on laws, contracts and economic rationality: reciprocity, moral obligations, duty towards community and trust are required, all elements stemming from a moral attitude rather than from rational calculation (Fukuyama, 1996, p. 24).

DOI: 10.1057/9781137467232.0007

The Keynesian trust, therefore, has a key role both in the economic and the social exchange, operating as a tool of regulation and order through the creation of social cohesiveness. As we have already mentioned, Keynesian trust is, first and foremost, institutional and systemic trust towards the government, that, through the role of warrant, ensures stability.

This is the key condition for economic, political, and social governance, allowing the irrational forces to be channelled towards positive ends of full employment.

To Keynes, the issue of employment, in fact, is tied to the trust factor: in 1933, Keynes wrote that the fundamental forces determining the volume of employment are the state of trust, the propensity to consume, the liquidity-preference and the quantity of money (Keynes et al., 1989, p. 126).

From these reflections, it is clear how the Keynesian trust represents the main weave of the social capital of a country. The Keynesian model of social capital follows the utilitarian definition of Coleman and regards the 'set of abilities, knowledge, capacities to affiliate with other individuals for economic but also social purposes. The ability to affiliate depends upon the degree in which communities share norms and values and by the ability to subordinate the interest of the individual to the one of the group' (Fukuyama, 1996, p. 23).

From these values trust emerges, bearing a very high social relevance, as being a generator of economic action. At the same time trust allows social interaction, propagating at a *micro* and *macro* social level through groups and social networks: if trust is inside the individual's behaviour, the social capital is inside the social relationships (Conte, 2009, p. 197). Social capital allows the sharing of an 'ethos' or *civicness* inside a group, a community and a social network (Peyrefitte, 1995; Fukuyama, 1996; Putnam, 2002). This notion may be related to the Keynesian duty, as social capital requires an absorption into the moral norms of a community by adhering to values such as integrity, honesty and reliability.

To better deepen the meaning of the role of social capital inside Keynesian thought, we need to clear a further aspect: social capital is a form of spontaneous sociality that could be found in the ability to create new affiliations and to cooperate inside the agreed terms of relationships. The fact that state intervention weakens the bottom–up developed communities doesn't separate at all the concept of social capital from Keynes' thought: the economist, in fact, argues that the State intervenes

DOI: 10.1057/9781137467232.0007

only according to the principle of good 'pater familiae' leaving to the individual the required freedom to express his or her creative energy and intervening only to avoid cyclical fluctuations and to preserve situations of social balance.

The government is the first to trust the individual, leaving the ground open to the entrepreneurship or initiative, as Keynes defines it, confiding in the innate abilities of the subject, and leading to spontaneous optimism.

In this sense trust is a social tool that benefits the community.

Notes

1   We refer to the modernization theories of Parsons (Parsons, 1965), to the static centre-periphery theory of Frank (Gunder Frank, 1967), and to the dynamic model of the 'world-system' of Wallerstein (Wallerstein, 1979).

2   The connection between the debt position of the USA and the credit position of China is an example of integration that Durkheim would define as 'organic'. This means that the roles of the two countries are reciprocally interlinked. Nevertheless, the strong position of the Asian giant in a polycentric and interlinked world could probably lead the country to play protagonist roles at a global level, also to protect its own interest: for instance, to protect European bonds previously bought, China may use its massive dollar reserve in different currencies owned by the country as a stabilizer of the economy: a role considered seemingly crucial by Keynes.

3   The International Monetary Fund (IMF) is an international organization that was initiated in 1944 at the Bretton Woods Conference and formally created in 1945 by 29 member countries. The IMF works to foster global growth and economic stability. It provides policy advice and financing to members in economic difficulties and also works with developing nations to help them achieve macro-economic stability and reduce poverty. Available at http://www.IMF.org, accessed 11 July 2014.

4   The Indignants Movement, and Take the Square #spanishrevolution, are a series of ongoing demonstrations in Spain whose origin can be traced to social networks such as Real Democracy NOW (Spanish: Democracia Real YA) or Youth Without a Future (Spanish: Juventud Sin Futuro) among other civilian digital platforms and 200 other small associations. The protests started on 15 May 2011 with an initial call in 58 Spanish cities. Available at Wikipedia, accessed 17 July 2014.

5   See Concluding Remarks, 'Supporting trust in the state of credit'.

DOI: 10.1057/9781137467232.0007

6   Roy Harrod (1939), Evsey Domar (1946) and Rosenstein-Rodan (1943) models.

7   Thomas Aquinas divided justice into two parts: commutative and distributive. The rules of commutative justice are precise and accurate. They concern the situations where one individual acts against another. The crime, the perpetrator and the victim are all identifiable to everyone. Distributive justice is 'loose, vague and indeterminate.' It cannot be reduced to rules and there is neither criminal nor crime when it is violated. Distributive justice involves the fulfilment of positive liberties, which are often costly. (Oswald, 2011).

8   As with capability, Amartya Sen intends what individuals are effectively able to do or to be; the set of the real chances that a person has to make his or her own life; the freedom to choose a specific behaviour (Federici, 2006).

9   Ferdinand Tönnies (1855–936), German sociologist whose theory reconciled the organic and social-contract conceptions of society.

10 Leon P. Laudatio, at the conferring of Honoris Causa Degree to Lord Robert Skidelsky, 16 February 2010, Università degli Studi di Roma Tre.

11 The Grameen Bank founded by M. Yunus has been the first bank in the world to provide loans to the poorest, not based on the principle of solvability, but rather based on the sense of trust.

DOI: 10.1057/9781137467232.0007

Concluding Remarks: The Economy of Trust Generates Value

Abstract: *The concept of 'Economy of Trust' has shown how trust, being an insuppressible instinct of the human condition, cannot vanish; it rather channels spontaneously towards entities of various origin. Padua introduces three different models of Economy of Trust: The Deregulated model; The Centralized model; The Selective model. This latter represents a moderate form of the Keynesian model of socialization as it allows the channelling of trust towards institutional bodies that are responsible for institutional trustworthiness, coordinating the national level with the international. This model would help the execution of five typologies of intervention to establish or re-establish trust in an economic and social context: Generating positive stories; Granting equity; Supporting trust in the state of credit; Determining the risk price; Entailing the sense of responsibility in media.*

Keywords: Centralized model; Deregulated model; Keynesian socialization; responsibility of media; Selective model; state of credit

Padua, Donatella. *John Maynard Keynes and the Economy of Trust: The Relevance of Keynsian Social Thought in a Global Society.* Basingstoke: Palgrave Macmillan, 2014. DOI: 10.1057/9781137467232.0008.

The only radical cure for the crises of confidence which afflict the economic life of the modern world would be to allow the individual no choice between consuming his income and ordering the production of the specific capital-asset which, even though it be on precarious evidence, impresses him as the most promising investment available to him. (GT, XII, VI)

At the end of this excursus on the role of trust in the economy and after examining the social implications of the speculation economy through the definition of Nominal Economy and Economy of Trust, we should seek to provide an answer to the questions: *How is it possible to build value via trust?* and, *How is it possible to get it back?*

In the state of recession following the 2007 slump, where early weak signs of recovery are being hailed, these questions lead us to reflect on how people may lose their scepticism and start to trust the new stories again – indeed, beliefs, positive stories, behaviours play a key social role, as they are able to generate self-generating spirals of trust, following the same pattern as the Mertonian self-fulfilling prophecy (Merton, 1968). The process results in a growing enhancement of trust.

According to the same perspective, Keynes believed in that spontaneous optimism feeding the resourcefulness to the benefit of collectivity, creating a climate of positive expectations. The latter are able, in turn, to trigger a self-generation of such a feeling. We have seen in Chapter 3 how Keynes teaches us how economic activity is founded on expectations. This fact is acknowledgeable today more so than yesterday: because of the complexity of the global financial system, the irrational component of trust becomes clearly preponderant, motivated by the inability to find a reliable basis to formulate estimates of prospective yields.

This represents a remarkable issue for policymakers, split between the use of monetary and fiscal policies to control the economic cycle, and the expectations of investors, entrepreneurs and managers. If the political economy may indicate long-term actions to grant stability and growth, the difficulty lies in keeping the expectations inside what Keynes calls 'financial convention' (expectations that circumstances won't vary indefinitely) high and positive. (Bateman and Davis, 1991): this determines the levels of investment at the base of economic and social growth.

The aim of this volume has been to design a framework of interactions between institutions – people – organizations, pointing out new levers

DOI: 10.1057/9781137467232.0008

which may be used to prompt positive expectations: the generation of such outcomes lie on policies of 'Economy of Trust'. This concept, in essence, explains the process of value building based on the exchange of products and services on a trust basis.

In this framework, the study has analysed how trust, being an insuppressible instinct of the human condition, cannot vanish; it rather channels itself spontaneously towards entities of varying origin. It is not said, in fact, that trust may be spontaneously directed to the institutions in authority to be trusted, that is, from which we expect them to be most trustworthy due to norms or on a social contract. During the 2007 economic crisis, we have seen how trust has been unconventionally directed towards other entities that have become strong and trustworthy *new powers*: financial companies, hedge funds, rating agencies, for instance.

For these reasons, by summarizing the concepts illustrated in this volume, we may introduce three different models of the Economy of Trust:

1 *The Deregulated Model*: in this model, trust is channelled spontaneously, upholding the principles of 'institutional', 'systemic' and 'interpersonal' trust, distributing towards various entities, such as financial companies and rating agencies (i.e., liberalism, monetarist economy);

2 *The Centralized Model*: trust is channelled towards a chief institution, assuring regulation. This is a mode of centralism typical of a centralized market reinforcing 'institutional' and 'systemic' trust (i.e., socialized Keynesian economy).

3 *The Selective Model*: free channelling of trust towards a number of institutions gaining trustworthiness at different levels: it is a form of regulated Economy of Trust within a free market (i.e., liberal economy with the presence of organizational bodies regulating institutional, financial, economic and social aspects).

This last model of Economy of Trust (Selective Model) represents a moderate form of the Keynesian model of socialization as it allows the channelling of trust towards institutional bodies (not only governmental bodies) responsible for institutional trustworthiness, coordinating the national level with the international.[1] For instance, in the Eurozone, the main trustable entities could be: the government of the specific country that has the role of the main country regulator; a central financial authority with full powers, including lending; and a European rating agency.

DOI: 10.1057/9781137467232.0008

These are already discussed topics within the topics difficult to be solved by the EU constituencies. However, they are particularly impactful in driving the Economy of Trust towards the purposes of building value in the most effective sense of its definition.

Indeed, this model would help the execution of five typologies of intervention to establish or re-establish trust in an economic and social context, as shown below.

Generate positive stories

We have already tackled how stories represent a tool used to give an interpretation of reality on which the individual builds his or her experience (Bruner, 1988).

We have observed from the Edelman Trust Barometer surveys how, during crises, trust towards companies is higher compared with trust in institutions, and how experts, academics and professionals are considered trustworthy even in a climate of distrust.

These facts lead us to highlight the need to generate stories grounded on 'tangible' impactful elements and able to generate discontinuity towards the past. An effectively communicated positive discontinuity may represent a driving force of institutional trust (Luhmann, 1979; Giddens, 1994) which may entail a positive reputation.

The high levels of trust the Italian President Mario Monti enjoyed in the early phases of his assignment[2] is a case in point: the new government had leveraged strong signs of positive discontinuity against Berlusconi's previous long-term government in terms of communication strategy, technical and pragmatic government approach, concreteness and speed of intervention. The signs of fostering trust and positive stories as being limited, direct and intelligible, have been perceived as almost-tangible.

Nevertheless, the Mario Monti 'technical government'[3] story soon came to an end with trust indexes severely dropping. After a year and a half of government, from 16 November 2011 to 28 April 2013, the Premier resigned. Apparently, his severe fiscal policy and foreign policy didn't meet the expectations of the people or the politicians and the technical government proved not to be able to cope with the complexity of internal politics. Moreover, the Monti government suffered at the peak of the economic global and national crisis, highlighted by the national financial indexes reaching an all-time-high negative national financial indexes.

DOI: 10.1057/9781137467232.0008

However, at its beginning, the Monti story appeared to be very promising: the Premier had gained the global policymakers' trust, leveraging
an academic past and a solid experience at the European Commission;
besides, he was head of the Anti-trust Committee at Bruxelles and
enjoyed a reputation of quick-decision maker: this story, based on a
positive reputation, was particularly relevant to the EU summit with
which President Monti had to deal.

As we have seen in Chapter 2, reputation tied to credibility, trust,
emotions, or to the synthetic transmission of an opinion, of a perception, is much faster than the transmission of money and, furthermore,
of goods. It is, in fact, an intangible good being transmitted by the
mechanisms of virality and it anticipates decisions working as a basis for
expectations.

In the Monti case study, trust virality had been triggered behind the
five trust beliefs. These were represented by 'competence' (acknowledged
by the 'technical' competence of the premier), 'benevolence' (belief that
sacrifices were supported for the safety of the country, of Europe and the
world, backed up by positive feedbacks from other European and over-
seas countries), 'transparence' (in public accounts, such as the parliamentary wages), and 'congruence of values' (recovery of the national image
in the world's eye). It is evident how these elements positively impacted
on trust indicators.

As already discussed, at any rate, trust builds on validations: the task
to lead a country is very complex in a systemic reality, as the current
and reconciling European objectives with the bonds of national needs
and expectations, appears to be a tough job. So, as trust decreases, the
financial spread increases and the Stock Exchange indicators drop, as
happened in April 2013, after the resignation of Mario Monti.

Granting equity

Apparently, The Nominal Economy lacks of the Simmelian's 'culture of
the exchange' (Simmel, 1987) as virtuality and the extreme volatility of
securities replacing cash don't allow forms of control and elude the creation of a social protection to secure the weakest.

In contrast, the Keynesian trust towards the State intervention may
evolve into a selective trust economy (the third model indicated above),
distributed across more entities, granting regulation and stability.

DOI: 10.1057/9781137467232.0008

Through these forms of institutional trust safeguarding the equity principles, a positive escalation of value generation may be triggered. This is due to the fact that interpersonal trust is tied to institutional trust – trust towards institutions, in fact, plays a great role in supporting social cohesion and order by stimulating the creation of relational bonds as social capital (Bourdieu, 1986; Coleman, 1990; Putnam, 1993). This favours the establishment of social cohesiveness and a positive climate for the development of cooperative relationships.[4]

In the current global market, where the rules of the game have changed, the intervention of institutions is probably not enough to grant trust: sympathy is needed even on a subsidiary basis.[5] The creation of a climate of trust towards the institutions in charge of regulating a democratic country, therefore, appears to be based on connecting a social justice which is linked to the economic exchange to a commutative justice and to a distributive justice which are responsible for the redistribution of wealth.

This concept highlights the relevance of including a 'risk redistributive justice' (in negative) as Ulrich Beck argues (Beck, 2000) within the culture of exchange, that is a justice operating with the aim to avoid wealth accumulation in higher social classes and risks at the bottom: hazards and insecurities induced and introduced by modernization. (Beck, 2000). It is worth remembering that the sense of equity is intimately tied to cooperation and trust[6] as it represents a very impactful social drive: people are willing to pay to punish those acting in a selfish way even if this implies an individual cost in the ratification of sanctions (Fehr et al., 2000): this means that citizens are ready to accept higher fiscal pressure if this succeeds in covering the costs of fighting fiscal elusion. This concept reflects in the same way that a judgement of equity may prevail upon rational economic behaviour (Kahneman et al., 1986).

Supporting trust in the state of credit

During crises, not only does the *speculator's trust* decline, but also trust towards the state of credit, that is, according to Keynes, the confidence of the lending institutions towards those who seek to borrow from them. However, 'whereas the weakening of either is enough to cause a collapse, recovery requires the revival of *both*. For whilst the weakening of credit is sufficient to bring about a collapse, its strengthening, though a necessary condition of recovery, is not a sufficient condition', (Keynes, 1978, p. 344): this implies that a recovery of trust on the part of the investors is needed.

DOI: 10.1057/9781137467232.0008

This is one of the huge monetary issues involving the political equilibrium within the Eurozone. A dampening of this issue may be operated by the introduction of a European lending institution. From this perspective, the decision by Standard & Poor's to downgrade to AA+, the European Financial Stability Facility's rating (the EFSF, as of July 2010, was permanently replaced by the ESM-European Stability Mechanism)[7] whose mandate is to safeguard financial stability in Europe, has created great uncertainty among investors.

The role of a new European institution as an ultimate lender would allow a higher confidence towards the state of credit and might trigger a growth trend on investments, with positive fallouts on the real economy. It has to be said however that, although in different forms, the ECB (European Central Bank) has implemented similar actions.[8]

Simmel, in his *The Philosophy of Money* (Simmel, 1987), illustrated how monetary credit trust in money is granted by the warrant role of the State and by collectivity that takes its value for granted. In the Nominal Economy, however, we have seen how during the systemic contagion of the 2008 global financial crisis, uncertainty, built up on the sovereign debts of some Eurozone countries, had negatively impacted upon the levels of trust on financial institutions. Moreover, in global finance, the existence of margin credits, which are variable according to the market situation, dampens down trust in the institutional state of credit in favour of interpersonal contingent relationships (Goffman, 2003; Garfinkel, 2004) and of new strong powers.

It is quite clear, then, how the stabilizing function of trust in the state of credit and in the speculator's investment activity, within a fragmented context, lacking solid central institutions, constantly depends on those organizations filling that institutional void of power.

This dynamic halts the creation of value in the form of social capital as being able to generate stable and productive network relationships (*bridging*) while respecting differences (Fontana, 2006), favouring, instead, profit greed.

Determining the risk price

Some economists argue that the subprime mortgage financial crisis may be interpreted as a mistake of investors on the evaluation of the price risk, that is, the economic and financial value consequent to the wrong evaluation of the risk. (The risk has a cost. The cost is the cost of the negative event!): in other words, the markets weren't allowed to perceive the correct 'risk price' based on the owned information. The crisis might have been avoided if banks and other regulating organizations would have managed adequately to determine the price of the risk (Skidelsky, 2010, p. 3).

In a context of uncertainty and of systemic risk on a global scale, it is understandable how difficult the task of determining the potential negative impact of a risk on the investment is. If, however, economics and law have such a task,[9] in the perspective of our discussion, we have to point out solutions based on 'trust'.

To grasp how risk management may be influenced by the trust factor, it is helpful to use the concept of the 'risk multiplier' that operates on a global scale in relation to the increase in wealth (Beck, 2000), and the 'trust multiplier' (Akerlof and Shiller, 2009, p. 31), which justifies the increase of trust thanks to virality and geometric progression.

The functioning of these two multipliers is moreover reinforced by the impact of technology on economic and social processes, generating new economic asymmetries with massive fallouts on the social side.

During the 2008 global financial crisis, it appeared clear how wealth management, founded on the science of economics (the sophisticated monetarists econometric models) and on digital information technology (digital highways and other secreted channels were financial information flows, and whose access is controllable), took over the control of the financial risk. Such a *selectivity of access and knowledge to the keys of risk* of global finance, as Beck maintains, has increased the asymmetry between the rich and the poor: there is, in fact, no need for transparency in a market where institutional investors and the few owners of wealth make exchanges between them without making the parallel market prices visible (Vegas, 2011, p. 42).

From these reflections it appears clear how actions to increase the level of transparency of some processes may lead to an easier determination of risk and, accordingly, operate a distribution or regulation of its control. Transparency is a component of trust. The accomplishment of this aim would favour a higher determinability of the risk price, avoiding systemic crises of the proportions we are still experiencing.

Entail the sense of responsibility in media

Mass-media has a huge impact on trust amplification generated by an effect that could be named 'trust in trust', in other words, behind the

DOI: 10.1057/9781137467232.0008

level of reliability on the communication medium. The media, in fact, represents an index of reliability per se. We have seen how, during the 2009 crisis the peak media trust index dropped to its all-time low levels, along with other indexes.

Media are called to have a strong sense of social responsibility. They play an extremely delicate role of influence in the multiplier effect of trust, or, vice-versa, of distrust: this result may lead, on the one hand, to generate cohesion inside society, amplifying positive effects, or on the other, trigger social fragmentation through the negative side-effects of mass distrust.

Just because they work on the collectivity, media greatly contribute to generating a climate of trust or distrust. This is the critical ground on which the multiplier's effects, stories, euphoria or panic peaks engage.

There are two main elements through which the media act: *agenda-setting*,[10] related to the selection of information newsworthiness; and the tone or level of tension created through the communication.

This latter, complying often with marketing strategies aiming at extreme forms of sensationalism of some news, acts on the individual's irrational perception, alerting the human sensors of risk.

If inspired by social purposes, media may reinforce trust during the times of crisis or recession, because of their powerful pervasiveness and engagement, contributing to a process of growth and development acceleration; we have seen, in fact, how the expectation of a positive result is an extremely powerful mechanism within the social and economic dynamic: by preceding a result that has not yet occurred in reality, it allows one to operate in anticipation, by realizing a process of synthesis which accelerates the dynamic of events between people, entrepreneurships and financial markets.

The above five points are to cover issues on how to build value on trust and how to get this feeling back. These synthetic answers, able to generate strong impacts both on the nominal and real sphere, offer points of reflection on the intrinsic economic value of trust.

At the end of these considerations, notwithstanding the complexity of the trust construct, a key aspect strongly emerges: the possibility, intrinsic to this feeling, to multiply its effect within the socio-economic fabric. We are referring to a 'lever-effect' that, thanks to a coordinated institutional action, may lead to geometrically exponential results.

In an interconnected global context, where the term 'asymmetry' has become the *leit-motiv* of the disruption of the western economic and social models of the 1990s institutions tend to orient themselves towards

DOI: 10.1057/9781137467232.0008

new tools to give an interpretation of phenomena. The comprehension of the Economy of Trust dynamics, through a sociological analysis, may represent an opening towards models founded on irrationality inspired by a re-evaluation of the thought of John Maynard Keynes.

Notes

1   The Keynesian economic policy, as we have evidenced in Chapter 1, is characterized by an assumption of organicity. Nevertheless, the Keynes' national economic policy, started in 1914 (Skidelsky, 1996, p. 150), doesn't fit a global context anymore. Keynesian policies, today, should be global or, at least involve global regions.

2   ISPO/3G Survey Deal & Research S.r.l, January 2012, Available at www. sondaggipoliticoelettorali.it, accessed 19 March 2012. The Mario Monti government lasted about one year and half, from 16 November 2011 to 28 April 2013.

3   A 'technical government' is Italian parliamentary jargon indicating a government without a political identity set up to rapidly face crisis situations. It is not submitted to the crossed vetoes of political parties.

4   Multifactor Productivity (MFP) relates output to a combined set of inputs. Bureau of Labour Statistics, available at www.bls.gov/mfp, accessed 16 July 2014.

5   The mutual relationship between economy and society cannot be reduced to just supply and demand. The 'Interdependence of Orders', a definition of Walter Eucken, a German economist father of ordoliberalism can only be understood if issues (*Beyond Supply and Demand* was the German title of the most well-known book of Wilhelm Röpke) are incorporated into the scientific analysis. This insight is fundamental for the concept of the Social Market Economy as conceived theoretically by Walter Eucken, Alfred Müller-Armack and Wilhelm Röpke, and put into political practice by Ludwig Erhard. Available at www.wipo.uni-freiburg.de, accessed 17 July 2014.

6   Werner Sombart (19 January 1863–18 May 1941) was a German economist and sociologist. He was the supporter of cooperative economics whereby the State plays a key role as an economic entity.

7   The European Financial Stability Facility (EFSF) provides financial assistance to the Euro area Member States, issuing bonds or other debt instruments on the capital markets. The EFSF was created as a temporary rescue mechanism. In October 2010, it was decided to create a permanent rescue mechanism, the European Stability Mechanism (ESM). The ESM came into force on 8 October 2012. As of 1 July 2013, the ESM is now the sole and permanent

DOI: 10.1057/9781137467232.0008

mechanism for responding to new requests for financial assistance by Euro area Member States. Available at http://www.efsf.europa.eu, accessed 10 June 2014.

8   By acknowledging that weak credit growth in the Euro area, particularly with small businesses, has been a major headwind for the recovery, the ECB Governor, Mario Draghi explained new monetary policy measures (Hearing at the Committee on Economic and Monetary Affairs of the European Parliament, Introductory statement by Mario Draghi, President of the ECB, Strasbourg, 14 July 2014). Available at: http://www.ecb.europa.eu/press, accessed 17 July 2014.

9   Some economists even auspicate the return of the Glass-Steagall law of 1933, which ruled out, on different bases, the production economy from the speculation economy.

10 The agenda-setting theory describes the 'ability [of the news media] to influence the salience of topics on the public agenda.' That is, if a news item is covered frequently and prominently, the audience will regard the issue as more important. The agenda-setting theory was formally developed by Dr Max McCombs and Dr Donald Shaw in a study on the 1968 presidential election. (McCombs et al., 2002).

DOI: 10.1057/9781137467232.0008

References

Adam, B., Beck, U. and van Loon, J. (2000) *The Risk Society and Beyond: Critical Issues for Social Theory*, Sage, London.

Akerlof, G.A. and Shiller, R.J. (2009) *Spiriti animali. Come la natura umana può salvare l'economia*, Rizzoli, Milano.

Arrow, K.J. (1951) *Social Choice and Individual Values*, Yale University Press,New haven.

Bak, P. and Chen, K. (1991) 'Self-Organized Criticality', *Scientific American*, 1, 264.

Barber, B. (1983) *The Logic and Limits of Trust*, Rutgers University Press, New Jersey.

Barry, B. and Hardin, R. (eds) (1982) *Rational Man and Irrational Society*, Sage, London.

Bateman B.W., Davis J.D. (1991), *Keynes and philosophy. Essays on the origin of Keynes's thought*, Edward Elgar Publishing LtD, Aldershot.

Bauman, Z. (2002) *Modernità liquida*, Editori Laterza, Roma-Bari.

Bauman, Z. (2003) *Voglia di comunità*, Laterza, Roma-Bari.

Bauman, Z. (2011) *Vite che non possiamo permetterci. Conversazioni con Citlali Rovirosa-Madrazo*, Laterza, Roma-Bari.

Beck, U. (2000) *La società del rischio. Verso una seconda modernità*, Carocci Editore, Roma [or. edn] (1986) *Risikogesellschaft. Auf dem Weg in eiene andere Moderne; Risk Society Revisited. Theory, Politics, Critiques and Research Programs*, Suhrkamp Verlag, Frankfurt am Main.

DOI: 10.1057/9781137467232.0009

Beck, U., Giddens, A., Lash, S. and Marrone, P. (1994) *Reflexive Modernization: Politics, Tradition and Aesthetics in the Modern Social Order*, Stanford University Press, Stanford.

Bendix, R. (1964) *Stato nazionale e integrazione di classe*, Laterza, Bari.

Benedetto XVI Pope (2009) *Caritas in veritate*, Libreria Editrice Vaticana, Città del Vaticano.

Beneduce, A. (1915) 'I problemi del rischio nella vita economica', *Giornale degli economisti e Rivista di statistica*, 1(2), 85–93.

Berra, M. (2007) *Sociologia delle reti telematiche*, Editori Laterza, Bari.

Blanchard, O., Amighini, A. and Giavazzi, F. (2011) *Macroeconomia*. Il Mulino, Bologna.

Boudon, R. (1970) *Metodologia della ricerca sociologica*, Il Mulino, Bologna [or. edn] (1969) *Les méthodes en sociologie*, Presses Universitarie de France, Paris.

Bourdieu P. (1986) The forms of capital, in J. G. Richardson (ed), *Handbook of theory and research for the sociology of education*, Grenwood Press, New York.

Bremmer, I. (2007) *The J Curve: A New Way to Understand Why Nations Rise and Fall*, Simon Schuster, New York.

Bruner, J. (1988) *La mente a più dimensioni*, Laterza, Bari.

Bruner, J. (1991) 'La costruzione narrativa della "realtà"', in M. Ammanniti and D.N. Stern (eds), *Rappresentazioni e narrazioni*, Laterza, Bari.

Caillè, A. (1998) *Il Terzo paradigma. Antropologia filosofica del dono*, Bollati Boringhieri, Torino.

Carabelli, A. (1988) *On Keynes's Method*, Macmillan, London.

Carabelli, A. (1991) 'The Methodology of the Critique of the Classical Theory: Keynes on Organic Interdependence', in Bradley W. Bateman and J.B. Davis (eds), *Keynes and Philosophy: Essays on the Origin of Keynes's Thought*, Edward Elgar Publishing Ltd, Gower House, UK.

Castells, M. (1996) *The Information Age: Economy, Society and Culture. The Rise of the Network Society*, Blackwell, Oxford.

Cesareo, V. (1990) *Elementi per uno scenario del mutamento culturale in Italia*, in V. Cesareo (ed.), *La cultura dell'Italia contemporanea. Trasformazione dei modelli di comportamento e identità sociale*, Fondazione Agnelli, Torino.

Coleman J.S. (1990), *Foundations of social theory*, The Blknap Press of Harvard University Press, Cambridge (MA)-London.

DOI: 10.1057/9781137467232.0009

Conte, M. (2009) *Sociologia della Fiducia. Il giuramento del legame sociale*, Edizioni Scientifiche Italiane, Napoli.

Cotesta, V. (1998) *Fiducia, Cooperazione, Solidarietà*, Liguori, Napoli.

Dilthey, W. (1949) *Introduzione alle scienze dello spirito*, Paravia, Torino.

Domar, E.D. (1941) *Essays in the Theory of Economic Growth*, Oxford University Press, Oxford.

Donati, P. (1991) *Teoria relazionale della società*, Franco Angeli, Milano.

Durkheim, E. (1999) *La divisione del lavoro sociale*, Edizioni di Comunità, Milano [or. edn] (1893) *De la division du travail social*, F. Alcan, Paris.

Edelman Trust Barometer (2011) available at edelman.com/trust/2011, accessed 20 January 2011.

Egidi, M. (2005) 'Logica della scelta e psicologia della decisione: un dualismo irrisolto', in M. Motterlini and F. Guala (eds), *Economia cognitiva e sperimentale*, EGEA Università Bocconi editore, Milano.

Elliott, L. (2011) 'Global Financial Crisis: Five Key Stages 2007–2011'. Available at: www.theguardian.com/business, accessed 7 August 2011.

Farina, M. (2011) *La storia riparte nel Mediterraneo 'Ma è un segno del declino'*, Corriere della Sera, La Lettura, 4 dicembre, 8.

Federici, M.C. (2006) *Dove fondano le libertà dell'uomo*, Borla, Roma.

Fehr, E. and Gachter, S. (2000) 'Cooperation and Punishment in Public Goods Experiments', *The American Economic Review*, 90(4), September, 980–994.

Fontana, R. (2006) *Uomini tra resistenza e resa. Genere, coesione e complessità sociale*, Guerini, Milano.

Fukuyama, F. (1996) *Fiducia. Come le virtù sociali contribuiscono alla creazione della prosperità*, Rizzoli, Milano.

Garfinkel, H. (1983) 'Che cosa è l'etnometodologia', in P.P. Figlioli and A. Dal Lago (eds), *Etnometodologia*, Il Mulino, Bologna, 55–87 [or. edn] (1967) *Studies in Ethnomethodology*, Englewood Cliffs, New Jersey, Prentice Hall.

Garfinkel, H. (2004) *La fiducia*, Armando, Roma.

Giddens, A. (1994) *Le conseguenze della modernità*, Il Mulino, Bologna [or. edn] (1990) *The Consequences of Modernity*, Cambridge, Polity Press.

Gunder Frank, A. (1967) *Capitalism and Underdevelopment in Latin America*, Monthly Review Press, Penguin Books, London.

Habermas, J. (1975) *La crisi di razionalità del capitalismo maturo*, Roma-Bari Laterza [or. edn] (1973) *Legitimationsprobleme im Spätkapitalismus*, Suhrkamp Verlag, Frankfurt am Main.

DOI: 10.1057/9781137467232.0009

Harrod, R. (1939) 'An Essay in Dynamic Theory', *Economic Journal*, 51, 14–33.

Hart, K. (1989) *Kinship, Contract and Trust*, Blackwell, Oxford.

Helburne, S. (1991) 'Burke and Keynes', in B.W. Bateman and J.D. Davis (eds), *Keynes and Philosophy: Essays on the Origin of Keynes's Thought*, Edward Elgar Publishing Limited, Aldershot, England, 30–54.

Irwin, N. and Paley, A.R. (2008) 'Greenspan Says He Was Wrong on Regulation', *Washington Post*, Friday, 24 October 2008, available at http://www.washingtonpost.com, accesed 10 August 2014.

Kaldor, N. (1939) 'Speculation and Economic Stability', *Ed. Review of Economic Studies*, VII, p.1.

Kahneman, D., Knetsch, J. and Thaler, R.H. (1986) 'Fairness as a Constraint in Profit Seeking: Entitlements in the Market', *American Economic Review*, 76, 728–41.

Keynes, J.M. (1937) 'The General Theory of Employment', *The Quarterly Journal of Economics*, 51(2), February, 209–223, The MIT Press Stable, available at http://www.jstor.org/stable/1882087, accessed 17 March 2009.

Keynes J. M. (1971-89), *The Collected Writings of John Maynard Keynes*, ed. by E. Johnson, D. Moggridge, 30 vols., The Macmillan Press LTD, London-Basingstoke, VII, p. 259.

Keynes, J.M. and Rymes, T.K. (1989) *Keynes's Lectures, 1932–35: Notes of a Representative Student (Keynesian Studies)*, Palgrave Macmillan, London.

Keynes, J.M. (2006) *Teoria generale dell'occupazione, dell'interesse e della moneta*, UTET Torino [or. edn] (1973) *The General Theory of Employment, Interest and Money*, 1st edn 1936. The Royal Economic Society 1973, 'The collected writings of John Maynard Keynes', vol. VII, London, Macmillan, 1973, pp. XXXV–412.

Kuhn, T.S. (1962) *The Structure of Scientific Revolutions*, 1st edn, University of Chicago Press, Chicago.

Lacohee, H.P., Cofta, P., Phippen, A. and Furnell, S. (2000) *Understanding Public Perceptions: Trust and Engagement in ICT-Mediated Services*, International Engineering Consortium, Chicago, USA.

Latouche, S. (2000) *La sfida di Minerva. Razionalità occidentale e ragione mediterranea*, Bollati Boringhieri, Torino.

Le Bon, G. (2004) *Psicologia delle folle*, TEA, Milano.

Lipset, S.M. and Schneider, W. (1983) *The Confidence Gap*. New York, Free Press.

DOI: 10.1057/9781137467232.0009

Lorenz, K. (1992) *L'Anello di Re Salomone*, Adelphi, La Nuova Italia.

Luhmann, N. (1979) *Potere e complessità sociale*, Il Saggiatore, Milano [or. edn] (1975) *Macht*, Ferdinand Enke Verlag, Stuttgart.

Luhmann, N. (2001) *Sistemi sociali. Fondamenti di una teoria generale*, Il Mulino, Bologna.

Luhmann, N. (2002) *La Fiducia*, Il Mulino, Bologna.

McCombs, M. and Reynolds, A. (2002) 'News Influence on Our Pictures of the World', in J. Bryant and D. Zillmann (eds), *Media Effects: Advances in Theory and Research*, LEA's communication series, 1–18, Mahwah, New Jersey, USA.

Magrassi, P. (2011) 'La faticosa strada della complessità nell'economia dell'impresa', *Harvard Business Review*, September, 61–5.

Marshall, T. (1976) *Cittadinanza e classe sociale*, UTET, Torino.

Maturana, H.R. and Varela, F.J. (1987) *L'albero della conoscenza*, Garzanti, Milano.

Mauss, M. (2002) *Saggio sul dono. Forma e motivo dello scambio nelle società arcaiche*, Einaudi, Torino.

Mayer, R.C., Davis, J.H. and Schoorman, F.D. (1995) 'An Integrative Model of Organizational Trust', *Academy of Management Review*, 20(3), 709–34.

McKnight, D.H. and Chervany, N.L. (1996) *The Meanings of Trust*, University of Minnesota, Minneapolis.

Merton, R.K. (1968) *Social Theory and Social Structure*, Free Press, New York.

Morin, E. (2001) *I sette saperi necessari all'educazione del futuro*, Raffaello Cortina, Milano.

Motterlini, M. and Guala, F. (2005) *Economia cognitiva e sperimentale*, EGEA Università Bocconi editore, Milano.

Mutti, A. (1998) *Capitale sociale e sviluppo. La fiducia come risorsa*, Il Mulino, Bologna.

Nash, J.F. Jr (1951) 'Non-cooperative games', *Annals of Mathematics*, 54, 286–95.

Ormerod, P. (2005) *Why Most Things Fail: Evolution, Extinction and Economics*, Faber & Faber, London.

Oswald, J. (2011) *Commutative and Distributive Justice*, available at http://azmytheconomics.wordpress.com, accessed 27 November 2011.

Padua, D. (2010) *Agire creativo e senso della razionalità in Pareto. Con una selezione di brani del Trattato di sociologia*, Franco Angeli, Milano

Padua, D. (2012) *Trust, Social Relations and Engagement. Understanding Customer Behaviour on the Web*, Palgrave MacMillan, London.

DOI: 10.1057/9781137467232.0009

Palley, T. (2009) *America's Exhausted Paradigm: Macroeconomic Causes of the Financial Crisis and Great Recession*, New American Foundation, Washington DC, 14–16.

Pansa, G. (2011) *Poco o niente. Eravamo poveri. Torneremo poveri*, Rizzoli, Milano.

Pareto, V. (1911) 'Rentier set speculateurs', *L'Indépendance*, 5, 157–66.

Parsons, T. (1965) *Il sistema sociale*, Ed. Comunità, Milano [or. edn] (1951) *The Social System*, Free Press, New York.

Pendenza, M. (2000) *Cooperazione, Fiducia e captale sociale. Elementi per una teoria del mutamento sociale*, Liguori Editore, Napoli.

Peyrefitte, A. (1995) *La société de confiance. Essai sur les origine set la nature du développement*, Editions Odile Jacob, Paris.

Poggi, G. (1998) *Denaro e modernità* La *'Filosofia del denaro' di Georg Simmel*, il Mulino, Bologna.

Prigogyne, I. (1986) *Dall'essere al divenire*, Einaudi, Torino.

Putnam R.D. (1993), *La tradizione civica delle regioni italiane*, Mondadori, Milano.

Putnam, R.D. (2002) 'Bowling Together', *The American Prospect*, 13(3), 11, February.

Rawls, J. (1999) *A Theory of Justice*, Oxford, University Press.

Ricœur, P. (2005) *Percorsi del riconoscimento*, Raffaello Cortina, Milano.

Rosenstein-Rodan, P.N. (1943) 'Problems of industrialization in Eastern and South-Eastern Europe', in *Economic Journal*, 53, pp. 202–11.

Santayana, G. (1923) 'Scepticism and Animal Faith', in *Realms of Being* (1927–1940), Charles Scribner's Sons, New York, USA.

Sen, A. (2001) *Lo sviluppo è libertà. Perché non c'è crescita senza democrazia*, Mondadori, Milano.

Severino, E. (2011) 'La vittoria delle tecnologie e la sfida a perdere tra economia e politica', *Corriere della sera*, 2 September, 18.

Simmel, G. (1987) *Filosofia del denaro*, A. Cavalli and L. Perucchi (eds), UTET, Torino [or. edn] (1900) *Philosophie des Geldes*, Leipzig.

Skidelsky, R. (1996) *Keynes*, Il Mulino, Bologna.

Skidelsky R. (2010), *The continuing relevance of Keynes, Lectio Magistralis*, on the occasion of the conferral of the honorary degree to Sir Robert Skidelsky, Università degli Studi Roma Tre, 16 February 2010.

Smelser, N.J. (1969) *Il comportamento collettivo*, Vallecchi, Firenze.

DOI: 10.1057/9781137467232.0009

Smith, A. (1995) *Teoria dei sentimenti morali*, BUR Rizzoli, Milano [or. edn] (1759) D.D. Raphael and A.L. Macfie (eds), *The Theory of Moral Sentiments*, Clarendon Press, Oxford.

Smith, A. (2010) *La ricchezza delle nazioni*, Newton Compton, Roma [or. edn] E. Cannan (ed.), *An Enquiry into the Nature and Causes of the Wealth of Nations* (1976), University of Chicago Press, Chicago.

Surowiecki, J. (2004) *The Wisdom of Crowds: Why the Many Are Smarter Than the Few and How Collective Wisdom Shapes Business, Economies, Societies and Nations*, Doubleday, New York.

Thrift, N. (1996) 'A Phantom State? International Money, Electronic Networks and Global Cities', in N. Thrift (ed.), *Spatial Formations*, Sage, London, 212–55.

Touraine, A. (1997) *Critica della modernità*, il Saggiatore, Milano [or. ed] (1992) *Critique de la modernitè*, Librairie Arthème Fayard, Paris.

Tremonti, G. (2012) *Uscita di sicurezza*, Rizzoli, Milano.

Trigilia, C. (1998) *Sociologia economica. Temi e percorsi contemporanei 2*, Il Mulino, Bologna.

Vegas, G. (2012) *Le regole premino l'economia reale*, Corriere della sera, 24 gennaio, 21.

Wallerstein, I. (1979) *The Capitalist World-Economy*, Cambridge University Press, Cambridge.

Weber, M. (1958) *Il metodo delle scienze storico-soci*ali, Einaudi, Torino.

Weber, M. (1968) *Economia e società*, Edizioni di Comunità, Milano.

Wilson, A. and Oosterveld, B. (2012) *Rating Action: Moody's adjusts ratings of 9 European sovereigns to capture downside risks*, available at https://www.moodys.com/research/Moodys-adjusts-ratings-of-9-European-sovereigns-to-capture-downside--PR_237716, February 2012. accessed 22 August 2014.

Zamagni, S. (2007) *L'economia del bene comune*, Città Nuova, Roma.

DOI: 10.1057/9781137467232.0009

Index

Beck, Ulrich, 96

Development vs. growth
current scenario, 89

econometric models, 7
Economy of Trust
socio-economic
development, 89
equity, 94
Eurozone crisis, 91

▶

Fukuyama, Francis, 91, 92, 99

institutions
depletion of powers, 90

justice
commutative, 95
distributive, social, 95

Keynes, John Maynard, 7
capitalism, 91
civilisation, 98
sociology, 99
optimism, 98
poverty, 93
redistribution
social dumping and law
dumping, 93
risk, 96
role of the government,
100

social capital, 100
socialisation, 91

Lehmann Brothers, 94
Luhmann, Niklas, 97

monetarist theory, 7

network paradigm
social networks, 100

Occupy Wall Street, 98

rationality
absolute rationality, 7
redistribution
risk, 95

Sen, Amartya, 96
capabilities, 99
Smith, Adam
invisible hand, 90
social cohesiveness, 93
Spence, Michael, 90

technology
technological economy, 94
techno-science, 92

uncertainty, 95
horizontal relationship, 98
unemployment
global, 92

CPSIA information can be obtained at www.ICGtesting.com
Printed in the USA
LVOW11*2325141114

413827LV00002B/10/P